Isaac Babel

Twayne's World Authors Series
Russian Literature

Charles A. Moser, Editor
George Washington University

TWAS 782

ISAAC BABEL
(1894-1941?)
Photograph courtesy of
Joan Daves Literary Agency

Isaac Babel

By Milton Ehre

University of Chicago

Twayne Publishers
A Division of G. K. Hall & Co. • *Boston*

. *Isaac Babel*

Milton Ehre

Copyright © 1986 by G.K. Hall & Co.
All Rights Reserved
Published by Twayne Publishers
A Division of G.K. Hall & Co.
70 Lincoln Street
Boston, Massachusetts 02111

Copyediting supervised by Lewis DeSimone
Book production by Elizabeth Todesco
Book design by Barbara Anderson

Typeset in 11 pt. Garamond
by Modern Graphics, Inc., Weymouth, Massachusetts

Printed on permanent/durable acid-free paper
and bound in the United States of America

Library of Congress Cataloging in Publication Data

Ehre, Milton, 1933–
   Isaac Babel.

   (Twayne's world authors series; TWAS 782)
   Bibliography: p. 159
   Includes index.
   1. Babel', I. (Isaak), 1894–1941—Criticism and
interpretation.   I. Title.   II. Series.
PG3476.B2Z655   1986   891.73'42   86–7650
ISBN 0–8057–6637–5

To the memory of
S. E., I. E., and J. E.

Contents

About the Author

Milton Ehre received his bachelor's degree at the City College of New York and his Ph.D. from Columbia University. He has taught at the University of Chicago since 1967, where he is now professor in the Department of Slavic Languages and Literatures. He is a former member of the editorial board of the *Slavic and East European Journal*. He has held grants and fellowships from the American Council of Learned Societies, the Philosophical Society, the National Endowment for the Humanities, and the Guggenheim Foundation. In 1984 he received a Fulbright-Hays-IREX grant, and was attached to the U.S.S.R. Academy of Sciences in Moscow as part of an exchange program.

Professor Ehre's major field of study is Russian literature of the nineteenth and early twentieth centuries. Among his publications are articles on Nikolay Gogol, Anton Chekhov, Mikhail Saltykov-Shchedrin, Evgeny Zamyatin, and Mikhail Bakhtin. He is also the author of *Oblomov and His Creator: The Life and Art of Ivan Goncharov* (1973) and editor and translator of *The Theater of Nikolay Gogol: Plays and Selected Writings* (1980). His translations of Gogol's plays have been widely performed, and he has recently completed a translation of Chekhov's *Uncle Vanya*, scheduled to be staged in the spring of 1986.

Preface

Isaac Babel (1894–1941?) wrote little, but he wrote well. In his all too brief career he created some of the finest short fiction in the history of Russian literature and one of the few undisputed masterpieces of the Soviet period. His great epic of the Russian Revolution, translated as *Red Cavalry,* is the classic treatment—at least in prose fiction—of that momentous event in human history. Later he fell victim to Stalin's reign of terror, and his work was suppressed. After the dictator's death he was rehabilitated, and three editions of his writings, none complete and all with some minor excisions, have appeared. Acclaimed in the 1920s as a leading figure of the new Soviet literature, he has again become a fitting subject for Soviet scholarship and criticism, though he still has not received the attention he deserves. He is highly regarded by the serious reading public. Since the appearance in 1955 of *The Collected Stories* in English translation with a groundbreaking essay by Lionel Trilling, American and English readers have also become acquainted with his work, and several monographs and numerous articles have been written about him. But then a writer of Babel's complexity and originality always leaves something new to be said.

This book is designed to meet the needs both of the general reader who may know little about its subject, and of the student of Russian literature who wishes to learn more about it. I discuss the works individually and in the context of the books or "cycles" in which they appeared, letting the texts guide my readings rather than, as has been fashionable lately, proceeding from a preconceived theory. Babel was a highly individualistic writer, not one to join schools or enlist in movements. The great Russian critic Yury Tynyanov asserted that every work of art is an "eccentric,"[1] a view that should make of criticism an inductive and tentative undertaking. Though genuine products of art are as unique as the men and women who make them, they still have things in common. In offering my interpretations, I emphasize two salient facts, simply because Babel cannot be understood without reference to them: that Babel was a Jew and that his writing displayed the loose and yet definable complex of tendencies that for want of a better name we still call "modernism."

Part of the research for this book was done at the Summer Research Laboratory of the Russian and East European Center of the University of Illinois at Urbana-Champaign and during a stay in the Soviet Union funded by a grant from Fulbright-Hays and the International Research and Exchanges Board (IREX). I express my gratitude for their assistance. Chapter 6, in a shortened and different form, appeared in the *Slavic Review* 40, no. 2 (June 1981).

Milton Ehre

University of Chicago

Chronology

1894   Isaac Babel born in Odessa on 13 July. Soon after, the Babel family relocates to Nikolaev. Studies English, French, and German; private Hebrew lessons.

1906   Enters the Nicholas I Commercial School in Odessa, where he writes his first stories in French.

1911   Enters the Institute of Finance and Business Studies in Kiev.

1913   First story, "Old Shloyme."

1916   Finishes his course of study. Takes up residence in St. Petersburg, where he begins to pursue a career as a writer. Maxim Gorky publishes several of his stories.

1917   Serves in the Russian Army in World War I.

1919   Serves in the Red Army in the Civil War following the Revolution. Marries Evgeniya Gronfein.

1920   Works as a journalist with the First Cavalry Army of the Red Army in the Polish campaign.

1921–1924   *Odessa Tales.*

1923   Death of his father.

1923–1925   *Red Cavalry.* Babel calls 1923 the true beginning of his literary career.

1925   His wife emigrates to Paris, his sister to Brussels. His mother emigrates the next year. First stories of the cycle *The Story of My Dovecot.*

1927–1928   Visits his wife in Paris.

1928   *Sunset,* a play.

1929   Daughter, Nathalie, born in Paris.

1930   Tours industrial sites and collective farms in the Ukraine in search of material on "socialist construction."

1931   Remainder of the *Dovecot* cycle.

Chapter One
Isaac Babel's Life

Jews in Russia

His first biographer said of Isaac Babel, in a phrase that sticks in the mind, that his literary sensibility was French, his vision Jewish, and his fate all too Russian.[1] History has forced the Jews of modern Russia to face a perilous issue of identity, asking them to what spiritual country they really belong. The policy of czarism was to eliminate the Jews as a national and religious entity in the Russian midst. Whereas medieval Muscovy had been relatively tolerant of its minuscule Jewish population, the emergence of an absolutist state threatened Jewish communal existence. Jews came to be regarded as a parasitic infestation of the Russian national body. Their expulsion from Russia proper began in the xenophobic reign of Ivan the Terrible (1547–84), and was codified into law by Catherine the Great (1762–96). Catherine annexed extensive territories in the West with large Jewish populations. Jews suddenly found themselves subjects of a foreign empire. Except for a privileged few, they were confined to a Pale of Settlement in mostly urban areas of the present-day Ukraine, White Russia, Lithuania, and Latvia.[2]

Illegal aliens within Russia, without civil rights in their crowded ghettos and villages, Jews were subject to harassment and legal disabilities designed, in the frank acknowledgment of the Council of State under Alexander II (the so-called "reformer czar"), "to destroy the exclusiveness of the Jew . . . , these communities forming in our land a secluded religious and civil caste, one might say, a state in a state."[3] The Jewish community suffered discriminatory taxation as well as restrictions on employment and on the right to own land. Punitive conscriptions for twenty-five-year terms into the army were a common occurrence (usually for vagrancy resulting from limitations on employment the government itself had imposed!). In the reign of Nicholas I (1825–55) conscription was also used to compel conversion of children from the age of twelve. Jews had to put up with periodic expulsions from lands where they

had lived for generations, quotas for admission to institutions of
higher learning, campaigns against the Talmud and other Hebrew
literature (including a public auto-da-fé of Hebrew classics in 1836).
Traditional Jewish dress was prohibited. The quarantine of the Jews
and their inferior legal status survived the reforms of the early years
of Alexander II (1855–81), the emancipation of the serfs in 1861,
and the abortive Russian experiment in limited parliamentary government (the Dumas) after 1905. Jewish emancipation came only
with the February Revolution of 1917.

The Jewish problem had reached crisis pitch by the time of Isaac
Babel's youth. The winds of modernism had reached even the most
isolated Jewish backwaters and expectations were on the rise. Russian
authority responded to the growing restiveness of the population,
both Gentile and Jewish, with its habitual reflex of increased repres-
sion. The regimes of Alexander III (1881–94) and Nicholas II (1894–
1917), frightened by the threat of revolution, retreated from the
reforms of their predecessor. The assassination of Alexander II had
inaugurated the fin de siècle in Russia. His heirs did not care to
follow in his footsteps. Reactionary social policies, extraordinary
police measures, chauvinistic nationalism and the anti-Semitism that
so often goes with it characterized political life at the turn of the
century. Jews made an easy scapegoat for the failures of the Russian
state, as well as for the revolutionary opposition its repressiveness
incited. Pogroms, tolerated by the central government and secretly
engineered by highly placed officials, became a regular feature of
Russian life.

The industrial revolution was in full swing in the Russia of the
1880s and 1890s and the change from a semifeudal to an emergent
capitalist society pauperized the Jewish community. It lost its traditional role as intermediary between gentry and serfs. As Jews
became workers and Christians became tradesmen, they entered into
direct competition for survival. Economic rivalry made Christians
susceptible to anti-Semitic demagoguery. The government's policy
of discriminatory legislation had taught them that ordinary law did
not apply to their Jewish countrymen. During the revolutionary
outbreaks of 1905 the government (or at least reactionary circles in
it) conspired to transform popular discontent into anger against the
Jews. Babel, then a child of eleven, witnessed (and as an adult
described) a massive assault against the Jews of his native Odessa
region which left over three hundred dead and thousands wounded

and maimed (how many women were raped we do not know). Economic disabilities created dismal poverty—it has been estimated that in the Pale of Settlement 40 percent of the Jewish population consisted of families of so-called *Luftmenschen,* persons with no reliable means of income;[4] ethnic and religious prejudice was a constant source of humiliation; the pogroms threatened the very physical existence of the Jewish community.

Over the course of the nineteenth century that community reacted in diverse and complicated ways to the onslaught upon its identity. Traditional Judaism drew into itself, striving to preserve age-old communal bonds, but often in ways that were dogmatic, legalistic, and obscurantist. Children were severely punished for the slightest breach of observance. The mere possession of a secular book was treated as a form of apostasy. Besieged by a hostile state and suspicious populace, Judaism also had to contend with internal revolts. The reformers of the Haskalah movement placed their hopes in education of their backward brothers and sisters, which would make them more acceptable to an enlightened absolutism. Antinomian and charismatic Hasidism preached joy in God's creation. Haskalah enlightener and Hasidic mystic, though radically opposed to each other, were yet united by the importance they assigned the individual and his personal relation to God. The former sought his moral perfection; the latter, his rebirth through mystic ecstasy. Both challenged the priority of the historic community insisted upon by traditional Judaism. Though only Hasidism had mass appeal, threatening at one time to engulf all East European Jewry, in the long run secularism proved the more potent force, but also brought in its wake consequences the more optimistic enlighteners had not foreseen. Denied the status of equals in the Russian empire, Jews found a sense of personal and national identity in their religion. Judaism's mythos of exile and promised return has since biblical times justified Jewish suffering. Secular values of effort and rewards to be won in this life undermined the meanings Jews had placed on their embattled lives. Rabbinical opponents of enlightenment, though too often ruled by blind prejudice, could also show an acute understanding of the Jewish predicament. A leader of the Haskalah, on a government sponsored trip to expound the blessings of education, heard the rabbis tell him: "So long as the Government does not accord equal rights to the Jew, general culture will only be his misfortune. The plain uneducated Jew does not balk at the low occupation of factor [agent of the gentry] or pedlar, for, drawing comfort and joy from his religion, he is reconciled to his miserable lot. But the Jew who is educated and enlightened, and yet has no means of occupying an honorable position in the country, will be moved by a feeling of discontent to renounce his religion. . . ."[5]

However, the lures of modernism proved irresistible. When the reforms of the 1860s opened educational opportunities, Jewish young people flocked to secondary schools and universities and, as their elders had feared, to the new ideologies of positivism, utilitarianism, and socialism. Though the mass of Jews remained conservative, placing their hopes in the benevolence of the czar, a significant number of the young joined the revolutionary movement. The ensuing strains on the Jewish family were enormous. Poverty and prejudice had denied the Jewish father the chance to participate actively in the larger world about him. It was all he could do to provide for his family, let alone freely shape his destiny. Some honed in themselves weapons of survival—the cunning and ironic skepticism of the ways of the world, examples of which fill the pages of Yiddish literature (and those of Isaac Babel). Others retreated to the hermetic security of the synagogue, unloading the burdens of the family on their wives. Now both mothers and fathers found themselves confronted by children who rejected the values upon which they had built their lives. A Jewish grandmother recalls:

We must now obey our children and submit completely to their will, just as once obedience to our parents was inviolable. As once with our parents, so now with our children, we must hold our tongues, and it is harder now than then. When our parents talked we listened respectfully, as now we listen, in pride and joy, as our chidren talk about themselves and their ideals. Our submissiveness and admiration make them tyrannize us. This is the reverse side of the coin, the negative impact of European culture on the Jews of Russia. No group but the Jews so swiftly and irrevocably abandoned everything for West European culture, and discarded its religion, and divested itself of its historical past and its traditions.[6]

Though Russians experienced a similar rift between "fathers and children," the isolation and deprivation of the Jewish community, combined with the rapidity of change, made its crisis particularly intense. Perhaps the Jewish tradition of Messianic expectation had fueled exaggerated hope. It was dashed by the pogroms and anti-Jewish legislation of the post-1881 period. For Jewish progressives the default of the Russian intelligentsia was even more traumatic. The People's Will, the organization of radical Russian populism, issued a leaflet applauding the revolutionary élan of rioters against Jews. To his credit, the only prominent figure of the Russian intelligentsia to denounce the pogroms of 1881 was Mikhail Saltykov-Shchedrin.[7] Such heroes of Jewish liberals as Ivan Turgenev and Leo Tolstoy remained silent, though Tolstoy did protest the later Kishinev pogrom of 1903. Fearing they no longer had a future in Russia, large numbers of Jews fled—to America, and also to the baptismal font. After the disintegration of the traditional Jewish community, conversion seemed to many the only route to participation in an evolving capitalist society.

Others began to nurture dreams of national renewal to counter the Russian nationalism that had excluded them. The years of Babel's youth, a time of profound insecurity and upheaval in the Jewish community, were marked by these contrary trends: on the one hand, a rush to assimilation; on the other, a heightened Jewish national self-consciousness. The quest for a specifically Jewish identity manifested itself in a revival of Hebraic culture, the flowering of Yiddish literature, and the appearance within Russian literature of writings concerned with Jewish life. Jews also organized themselves into nationalist movements, the most important of which were Zionism and the socialism of the Jewish Labor Bund. Zionism sought statehood; the Bund defined the Jews as a culturally autonomous people within the multinational Empire. Heatedly antagonistic, Zionism and Bundism both scorned assimilationism and traditional Jewish resignation to suffering. The revulsion against Jewish passivity we shall discover in Babel's fiction was by no means an isolated instance among Jews of his generation.

A Jewish Family

Of the possible responses to secularization and persecution the Babel family chose the way of assimilation.[8] The family history is a common one of a casual drift away from Jewish traditions. Isaac's paternal grandfather pursued rabbinical studies; his paternal grandmother's native language was Yiddish and she spoke Russian with difficulty. His parents still used Yiddish but only between themselves, addressing the children in Russian. To learn the native language of his parents and grandparents Isaac had to turn to the working-class children of Odessa. His grandparents scrupulously observed the articles of their faith; his parents observed only the High Holy Days of Rosh Hashanah and Yom Kippur, and celebrated the Passover, though they kept kosher. As was customary for Jewish boys, Isaac from the age of ten attended a religious school in addition to secular school, and also received private Hebrew lessons from a tutor. As a teenager he belonged to a Jewish welfare organization (youthful idealism also drew him briefly to Tolstoyism). Nevertheless, he grew up to consider himself an atheist.

"As a little bit of musk fills an entire house," the poet Osip Mandelstam ruminates, "so the least influence of Judaism overflows all of one's life."[9] Though faith failed Babel—he wrily swears by the "ex-God" in his letters—he never severed his cultural connections with his Jewish heritage. The one Jewish holiday he always celebrated, however informally, was Passover, when Jews remember their deliverance from bondage as a free nation. He was disappointed when his wife named their daughter Nathalie, preferring a Jewish name. Yiddish literature interested him—he worked as an editor on the complete edition of Sholom Aleichem's works, and at the height of the great purges, when he must have suspected his days were numbered, he spent evenings reading that genial comic writer "in *our* highly original tongue."[10] The pithy aphorisms of Yiddish literature and speech, its self-effacing ironies that barely conceal latent assertion, influenced his style, as did the cadenced intonations of the Torah and prayer book. Repudiating the insularity of the Jewish ghetto to join the mainstream of Russian and European culture, he felt nostalgia for the warmth of Jewish family life. More important, his Jewishness is a central subject of his art.

Odessa

The erosion of traditional belief in the Babel household would have come as no surprise to East European Jews when they heard the family was from Odessa. In Jewish folklore the cosmopolitan city on the Black Sea is a Sodom of apostasy, frivolity, and sin. It was a new city for newcomers, without the weight, burdensome or benign, of tradition. From its beginnings (it was incorporated into the Empire only in 1794) Odessa was a place of escape, where men and women could make a fresh start. Runaway serfs flocked to this bustling city, which never knew a serf economy, as did bankrupt gentry, Jews (including Babel's forebears) fleeing their suffocating villages, Bulgarians, Croats, Serbs, and Albanians fleeing Turkish oppression, Greeks, Italians, and Armenians seeking to employ their trading skills to advantage, adventurers of all stripes hoping to strike it rich. Odessa was a city on the make. As the granary of southern Russia and the major outlet for Russian trade with the Middle and Far East, the city grew rapidly into the second busiest port of the Empire (after St. Petersburg) and its fourth largest city (after St. Petersburg, Moscow, and Warsaw).

Without the somber dignity of medieval Moscow or the cool elegance of imperial St. Petersburg, Odessa was the most bourgeois of Russian cities, "an European oasis in feudal Russia," as Russian historians have called it. Like any large city it had its pockets of squalor. The crowded Jewish ghetto of Moldavanka, a favorite subject for Babel, was a hotbed of crime. Overall, though, Odessa presented an attractive face. It was recent enough to have been built according to plan, which resulted in a city of open and generous appearance. Shade trees and rows of tidy limestone houses lined paved streets (a rarity in nineteenth-century Russia) and broad boulevards. The most elegant among them, the Primorsky (formerly the Nicholas), faced by handsome mansions, sweeps down to the sea by way of the Potyomkin steps. The architecture of the Old City is a flamboyant mix of styles ranging from Florentine Gothic to Viennese Baroque. Numerous plazas and parks offer ample space for outdoor concerts and operas. Gracious private villas once studded the heights overhanging the sea.

What it lacked in historical tradition Odessa made up for with southern geniality. This Russian Marseilles exuded the casual bonhomie of a Mediterranean city. A rich mélange of humanity could be found strolling along sunny beaches or crowding its many restaurants and cafés: sailors and traders from foreign ports, the ambitious and hopeful attracted by its opportunities, vacationers from dreary northern winters drawn by warm southern skies, the sick and tired come to restore their energies at the local spas. Just as Babel celebrated its color and vibrancy in the twentieth century, so his great predecessor, Alexander Pushkin, had sung its praises in the nineteenth:

> There for a long time skies are clear.
> There, stirring, an abundant trade

sets up its sails.
There all exhales, diffuses Europe,
all glitters with the South, and brindles with live variety.
The tongue of golden Italy
resounds along the gay street where
walks the proud Slav,
Frenchman, Spaniard, Armenian,
and Greek, and the heavy Moldavian. . . .[11]

The animation of its streets was complemented by the vitality of
its cultural life. Art often thrives in cities large enough to be cosmopolitan but small enough to nurture a feeling of community, as
Periclean Athens and Elizabethan London attest. Odessa had a lively
press in several languages for its polyglot population, in addition
to a university, libraries and museums, and busy theaters. Italian
opera was a major attraction (the baroque opera house is one of the
finest in the country). Music throve. The city has been a breeding
ground for virtuousi, many of them Jewish: Mischa Elman, Jascha
Heifetz, Efrem Zimbalist, Osip Gabrilowitsch, David Oistrakh,
Emil Gilels, Svyatoslav Richter. More susceptible than other Russian
cities to foreign fashion, Odessa gave an early welcome to popular
commercial literature—adventure tales, melodramatic potboilers,
romances. Port cities bring strangers together with stories to tell,
and the city was famed for its love of the anecdote. An interest in
simulation of oral narration, or what Russians call *skaz,* a touch of
"southern romanticism," and salty humor are characteristic of the
many outstanding Soviet writers Odessa produced, causing Babel
and others to speak of an "Odessan School," or a "Southern School"
of Soviet literature *(I,* 401–2). Eduard Bagritsky, Valentin Kataev,
Ilya Ilf and Evgeny Petrov, Konstantin Paustovsky, and Yury
Olesha are all identified with Odessa, and Mikhail Zoshchenko,
from Poltava, is considered part of the southern wave.

In 1904, one third of Odessa's half million residents were Jews.
They contributed much to the spiritual life of their country, and
also created an intellectual and cultural milieu of Jewish character.
The direction of their activity, in tune with the city's cosmopolitan
climate, was strongly assimilationist. Odessa's commercial opportunities and the absence of the stifling legacy of serfdom permitted
a significant number of Jews to rise to the middle class. With
prosperity came the desire to belong. The Jews of Odessa produced

a culture of the surface, largely innocent of the depths of suffering and the flights of Messianic hope of their brethren in the poverty-stricken border territories to the west. The first Jewish school for secular education opened as early as 1826, and the city quickly became the center of the Haskalah Enlightenment, and later of a Russification movement. Though Russification coincided with the government's policy of obliterating the culture of Jews and other minorities, the movement ran into trouble for having the temerity to advocate civil rights as a concomitant of assimilation. *Rassvet* (Dawn), the first Jewish journal in the Russian language, did not survive the year of its birth (1860) because of censorship difficulties; its successors met a similar fate. Nevertheless, upwardly mobile Jews did not easily abandon their hope of joining the Russian nation as equals. The soil for assimilation was so fertile in Odessa that a group of Jewish intellectuals went so far as to urge the substitution of Russian for Hebrew in prayer books, a proposal that, had they heard it, would have sent shivers down the spines of the Jews of the ghettos and villages.

As so often in Jewish history, the best friends of Jewish nationalism were its enemies. The pogroms of 1871, 1881, and 1905 cooled the ardor of the Russifiers. Shoots of Jewish nationalism sprang up in the city. A growing Jewish proletariat of longshoremen and industrial workers was more inclined to defend itself than were their ambitious petit-bourgeois cousins. Jewish university students were swept up by the revolutionary passions that culminated in the upheaval of 1905. The Jews of Odessa were the first in the Empire to organize themselves for self-defense against anti-Semitic rioters. In his fiction Babel distinguishes sharply between the Jew who submits and the Jew who resists.

An Odessan Artist

Men and women feel one way in times of crisis, another way in times of peace. In his memoir of Odessa written on the eve of the Revolution, it is its comfortable, middle-class spirit that Babel remembers fondly. Odessa, he writes, is a city of the sun, of fecundity and material well-being. The Jews give the city "its light-hearted and sunny atmosphere, . . . and the Jews are a people who are very emphatic about some very simple things. They marry so as to live through the ages, save money to buy houses and give their wives astrakhan jackets. They are very fond of their children because it's very nice to love one's children, and necessary too."[12]

This southern geniality and bourgeois coziness become for the young Babel the basis of an artistic credo. Russian literature has not yet had "a real, joyous, and clear description of the sun," he argues. Instead of exercising its muscles in the clear daylight of sensuous physical life, it has chosen to dwell in disembodied mists— Turgenev's elegiac nature, his "dewy morning, the still of night," or "the dense and mysterious fog" of Dostoevsky's St. Petersburg. "These drab roads and shrouds of fog have smothered people, distorting them in a manner that is at once comical and terrible," he writes, adding that more recent attempts at ethnographic naturalism are "the same old story"—portraits of a Russia that is bleak, savage, and boring to read about.[13]

The Odessan is a child of the sun and also of the sea, a dreamer whose "heart thirsts for beautiful and new lands." The Odessan writer prefers tangible experience to abstraction, and he also has a penchant for the exotic. He need not let his imagination roam over the sea to distant places, for he clothes the familiar in romantic color (I, 401–2). In the history of Russian literature Babel finds a model for a richly textured literature of common life only in Gogol, and then not the St. Petersburg Gogol of urban grotesquery, but the playfully humorous and lushly romantic "southern" Gogol of the Ukrainian tales. Among contemporary writers only Gorky understands the value of healthy, exuberant life, but even so his appreciation is merely "cerebral." Gorky's sun beckons to him from the future. It is a project, not a presence.[14]

To find a true poet of the sun Babel turns his back on the metaphysical urgencies and social pathos of Russian literature, looking instead to France and especially to Guy de Maupassant. In some ways it is an odd choice. Babel's prose can be ornately baroque; while Maupassant's is sober and unspectacular; Babel is morally earnest and Maupassant is a sophisticated entertainer. Nevertheless, the Frenchman's skill in presenting the surface of things appealed to Babel. Maupassant, he maintains, is a writer of daylight actualities rather than mystic night. He shows and does not tell. A carriage clattering down a heat-scorched road, a fat sly youth, a strapping peasant girl—"What they're doing there, and why, that's their own affair. The sky is hot and the earth is hot. . . . That's all there is to it."

If Russia is to produce a muscular prose of the outdoors, of the play and color of variegated physical life, Babel believes it will come from Odessa: "Above all, this city has the material conditions to nurture the talent of a Maupassant. Summers at its bathing spots there glisten in the sun the bronzed muscular figures of young men busy at sports, the powerful bodies of fishermen not busy at sports, the fat, potbellied, and good-natured bodies of traders; one finds pimpled and scrawny dreamers, inventors, brokers."[15]

Babel's program for Russian literature amounts to a democracy of the flesh. He rejects the individualism of the nineteenth-century novel, whether bourgeois or aristocratic, which centered its attention on the mind of a hero engaged in an intellectual and spiritual quest—the Raskolnikovs of Dostoevsky, the Pierres and Levins of Tolstoy. In its place he proposes a biological naturalism enriched by the romantically picturesque.

Babel did not become the kind of writer he imagined Maupassant to be (the Frenchman's cynicism seems to have escaped him). The cataclysm of the Russian Revolution destroyed the grounds for a stable middle-class society necessary for such an amiable literature. Dark years lay ahead. The experience of revolution and the bloody civil war that followed on its heels brought Babel face to face with the brutality of our century. His service with the Red Army in the Polish campaign of 1920 introduced him to a world radically different from that of comfortable Odessa. The battleground was the western Ukraine (Galicia, Podolia, Volhynia), which ever since the seventeenth century had been the scene of political turmoil and ethnic hatreds. Violent Cossacks, poor and often rabidly anti-Semitic Ukrainian peasants were something new for Babel, as were, indeed, the masses of his own people. Having spent his youth among Odessa's ambitious salesmen and crafty hustlers, its complacent burghers and their sleek fur-clad wives, he was shocked by the Jews of the western Pale of Settlement. Here Jews lived huddled in bleak villages and dingy ghettos, desperately struggling to avoid ruin and starvation, their lives under constant threat from the surrounding sea of enmity. Spiritual life, both religious and secular, had an intensity unknown in Odessa, as the peril of their situation drove Jews to seek the security of century-old traditions or to dream of millenial deliverance. Babel's program for a "sunny" literature resulted in the charming but limited *Odessa Tales,* whereas his confrontation with suffering gave birth to his sole great book, *Red Cavalry*.

Childhood

Just as the world proved darker than his early literary manifesto allowed, so Babel's childhood was more problematical than his portrait of cheerful Odessa would suggest. In a cycle of stories intended to appear under the title of one of them, "The Story of My Dovecot" (1925)—the others are "First Love" (1925), "Awakening" (1931), and "In the Basement" (1931)—Babel gives us a picture of what is ostensibly his family. Two of the stories are set during the pogroms accompanying the Revolution of 1905, when the Babels were living in Nikolaev, some eighty miles from Odessa. In "First Love" the child, the central figure of the cycle, spots his distraught father, whose store has just been pillaged by a mob: "I saw through the window the empty street and my redheaded father walking along in the roadway. He walked bareheaded, his soft red hair fluttering, his paper dickey askew and fastened to the wrong button." The father implores help of a Cossack officer. "The officer murmured something and again put the lemon glove to his cap. . . . My father crawled in front of the horse on his knees, rubbing up against its short, kindly, tousled legs" *(I, 222–23)*.

To compensate for his impotence the father has devoted his life to achieving middle-class respectability, and has burdened the frail shoulders of his sole son with enormous ambitions. The son, he dreams, will some day vindicate his own frustrations. The long suffering mother (in "The Story of My Dovecot") is aware of her husband's vanity and fearful of its consequences. A life of poverty has made her wary: "She looked at me with bitter compassion, as one might look at a cripple, because she alone knew what a family ours was for misfortune. . . . She had never been dazzled by her husband's pauper pride, by his incomprehensible belief that our family would one day be richer and more powerful than all others on earth." She is protective of her son and, the story suggests, seeks an intimacy from him her self-absorbed husband and an assortment of eccentric male relatives cannot provide—"And so I alone of all our family was left to my mother"*(I, 211–12)*.

To what extent may this fictionalized family be identified with Babel's real family? The details, his daughter Nathalie tells us, are wrong.[16] Emmanuel Isaakovich Babel was not a storekeeper. Nor was he poor, at least not at the time of his son's birth. Babel's father worked as a sales representative for a manufacturer of agricultural machinery, a major industry of the Odessa region. In 1905 he went into business for himself, purchased a warehouse, and opened an office on Politsiskaya Street, where export-import firms were located. He was a merchant of the first or second guild, the highest status for merchants in the feudal rankings of Russian society. His position and his prosperity were his own achievements. Certain doors had opened only recently for Jews, and the Babels and the Shvevels, his wife's family, had moved to Odessa from elsewhere in the Ukraine to take advantage of them.

Isaac was born in Moldavanka, a seedy suburb of Odessa, on 13 July 1894, and a little later Emmanuel moved his family to more pleasant surroundings. In Nikolaev the Babels enjoyed a garden, a dovecot, and a courtyard that served as a skating rink in winter. These were quite comfortable circumstances for the time, better than most Jews (or Russians) could hope for. A daughter, Meri, was born here in 1899, but Isaac, as the son and the oldest child, remained the favorite. In 1905 Emmanuel returned his family to Odessa. He may have decided on the move because the city, with its large Jewish population, seemed safer in this dangerous year of revolution and anti-Jewish disorders, or simply because it offered better business opportunities for himself and more educational choices for his growing children. For a while Isaac lived with his maternal grandmother and two aunts, one of whom was a dentist—the family as a whole seems to have been steadily climbing into the middle class. When the Babels found a permanent apartment, it was on one of the finest streets in Odessa.

Emmanuel's personality was strikingly different from that of the harried father of the *Dovecot* tales. The face he presented to the world was of a successful man of business, "dandyish, elegant, good-looking, . . . a man of imposing physique and impetuous nature."[17] As the family's poverty was a myth of Isaac's invention, so was the story of its victimization in a pogrom. The pogrom occurred, of course, the impressionable young Isaac witnessed its violence and was deeply affected by it, but the Babels escaped unscathed.

But the fiction must tell its own truth. There are writers—Dickens, Zola, Chekhov—who are sociologists of the imagination. Their sufferings and desires may attend the act of writing, but these

blend imperceptibly into a mimesis of historical reality. They seal
their characters behind the walls of a fictional world whose claim
to objective reality is so strong that, though we may do so with
profit, we do not feel compelled to seek out the author's soul lurking
behind the window. Babel does not belong to their company. A
powerful strain of lyricism runs through his work. It is no hap-
penstance that his narratives are almost always in the first person;
his favorite plot, the sentimental education of a young man, Jewish
and a writer, in the ways of the world. This is not to say that Babel
is a confessionalist. Like any worthwhile writer, he struggles to
transmute personal experience into the universalized forms of art,
and it comes as no surprise when the details of his fiction depart
from his biography (which we know through witnesses who may
have their own biases). But neither is he a realist pretending to
picture a milieu from which the subjective self has been effectively
excluded. Much of his fiction takes the form of a biography of his
soul, and the sense of a personal crisis hovers almost constantly at
its edges. Try as he might Babel could never turn himself into the
genial portraitist of the *comédie humaine* he imagined his hero Maupassant to be. His inner life was too pressured, the age too tragic.

The tale that Babel tells in the *Dovecot* cycle (and in transformed,
symbolic ways in *Red Cavalry*) is that of a child oppressed by his
father's ambition and disillusioned by his weakness, drawn to his
mother (and other maternal figures) for comfort before rebelling
against both to seek alternative images of manhood and an escape
from dependency. It is a story common to cultures and sub-cultures
where men are deprived of normal outlets for assertion and as a
result retreat into passivity or decide that they can prove themselves
only through extraordinary achievement.

Emmanuel Babel, though by no means the pathetic father of the
fiction, did not escape the common insecurity. The sources are scanty
and differ, but they suggest that under the respectable and polished
surface his share of human turmoil was concealed. Nathalie Babel
admits that his "rages were legendary." Of the two available memoirs by people not belonging to the Babel family, one mentions
him merely as a respected salesman of agricultural equipment, while
the other describes a melancholy man whose heart was not in "his
long unprofitable business" (Nathalie merely says the business had
its "ups and downs," which is more plausible, given the family's
comfortable situation during Isaac's early years.) Disappointed in

his business, our source continues, Emmanuel would spend his spare hours writing "satirical observations" in which he ridiculed "the worldly vanity of his neighbors." Emmanuel cherished the dream of the upwardly mobile—that his son Isaac, the apple of his eye, would rise not only above his neighbors, but would do better in life than he had. A career in business was not good enough for him; he must distinguish himself in the world of culture. "One of his ambitions," Nathalie writes, "was to educate his children as well as possible—especially his son for whom he had a scarcely concealed preference. Nothing was too good for the boy. For Emmanuel Babel education meant that his son must speak a number of foreign languages, study music and Hebrew."[18] His legacy to his son, it would seem, was the very Jewish conviction that what counts in the long run is the life of the Word.

Parents nurture and protect their children, and also transmit the values of their culture. Isaac's relation to his father and to his Jewishness was complicated. Like his fictional persona he too rebelled to choose a life of action—as soldier, Cossack warrior of sorts, horseman (horses were Babel's lifelong passion). If he fulfilled his father's dreams of intellectual accomplishment by becoming a writer, he was an unconventional one. Throughout his career Babel resisted settling into the role of a professional writer. He despised literary talk, often slipping away from his educated friends to rub elbows with jockeys, prostitutes, old army pals, tough Communist commissars, even ruthless agents of the Cheka (the secret police).[19] Rejecting Jewish subservience, hostile to a life too exclusively centered on the mind, he also indicted Jewish remoteness from nature: "The spirit of my ancestors has risen up in me against one of Papa's rules—to stay clear of nature. . . ." A frail boy—he suffered from asthma, was nearsighted and nervous—he longed to enjoy the pleasures of the body, to sport in the sun with those muscular youths of Odessa. He fled school to play billiards in Greek coffee houses, drink wine in Moldavanka's taverns, and feel the excitement of a vibrant port city. Learning to swim came to seem more crucial for his personal growth than musty Hebrew books and boring violin lessons: "In my childhood, chained to Gemara, I had led the life of a sage. When I grew up I started climbing trees."[20]

Yet he was very much his father's son. As he wrote to his mother in 1927, four years after his father's death:

I am not one of those you can bend into a ram's horn. I feel well and I
still hope to do things in the world. So why should she [his sister] be in
a "desperate" mood? Why all this pitiful whimpering? Why all this
neurotic imbalance? Keep your chins up, damn you, pull your bellies in,
and forward, march! What a moaning crew! There is actually no reason
for you to moan. When I go through moments of despair, I think of Papa.
What he expected and wanted from us was success not moaning. . . .
Remembering him, I feel a surge of strength, and I urge myself forward.
Everything I promised him, not in words but in thought, I shall carry
out, because I have a sacred respect for his memory. And it hurts me to
think you should drown the only sacred memory I have in your needless
tears and weakness.[21]

If Babel rejected some of his father's values, he identified with others.
He too was ambitious; and his ambitions, following the course of
his father's educational program, lay in the field of culture. His
stoic sense of duty, which carried him through more than the usual
quota of life's difficulties, was an inheritance from his father. Scorn-
ing petit-bourgeois conformity to pursue the unattached career of
an artist, now and then striking out on adventures and courting
danger, he remained, as he described himself, "a classically Jewish
'family man.' . . ." At loose ends without his family after his wife,
mother, and sister emigrated in the mid-twenties—he constantly
urged them to return, expressed anxious concern about their welfare,
and was "fully afflicted with that family trait of 'worrying.' "[22]
    Worrying was his mother's (and sister's) department. Of all his
family, he once wrote, only he and his daughter "have any talent
for gaiety." All his life Babel struggled to free himself from the
anxious self-pity he complained of in his mother.[23] He identified
with his father's stoicism as one way to keep his footing in the
swamps of sadness, or else determinedly cultivated joy. Gaiety became an ethical principle for him. "I wish you joy," he would sign
his holiday greetings, "as much joy as possible; there is nothing
more important in the world."[24] The public Babel was witty and
urbane, playfully ironic, fond of good talk and good jokes, an
Odessan lover of the anecdote.
    Joy did not come easily; it had to be worked at. At some point
in his life Babel seems to have resolved to turn himself into a pillar
of strength. Facing the world with an untroubled countenance may
have been a way to dissociate himself from his father's fears of failure,
or to demonstrate to his anxious mother that she could rely on him.

He assures her that she had given birth to "an unbending and full-blooded warrior." "I am made of a dough that is a mixture of stubbornness and patience and it is only when these two elements are strained to the utmost that *la joie de vivre* comes over me," he wrote. We live "for the affirmation of our personal pride and worth."[25] Self-pity was not in his line. Though he lived in horrendous times of war, revolution, and state terror, he seldom complained. His contemporaries respected him for his talent, his exceptional intelligence, and his dignity. There is hardly a memoirist who fails to mention his penetrating eyes, perpetually observant—"a writer must have curiosity and wonder," he said[26]—and sparkling with the bemused irony of a man keeping his distance. Though gregarious, he fenced off large areas of private reserve. He was determined to keep his sufferings to himself. The strain showed in the form of chronic nervousness and a certain fussiness.

On one occasion Babel flared up at his mother: "Do you still know how to look after children and do they let you? Do you shove a grimy pacifier into your granddaughter's mouth as you used to do with your son?. . . . Do you chew a day-old bagel with seeds on it with your gums and then give it to her wet with saliva as you used to do with your son? for which he will never forgive you. And then too, you begrudged me diapers, you didn't give me orange juice, you rocked your son in a cradle, killing his self-reliance. . . ."[27] This teasing of the woman's old world ways is cruel but uncharacteristic. Babel charged his mother with being at once stinting and overly solicitous, and thereby destroying his self-confidence. He knew he had something to prove. Nevertheless, we may wonder how accurate the portrait is and how much weight we should give to his accusations. It is in our nature to fret that we weren't loved enough or properly. To express such anger openly required him to have considerable confidence in the solidity of their relationship. His mother may not have been exactly his "great love on this earth," as he once called her,[28] but he was deeply attached to her. If the fiction leads us to expect an element of neurotic dependency, it does not show in the correspondence, where he usually shows manly respect and affection. Babel suffered his share of conflicts and pressures in his childhood, but he also acquired from his family a good deal of strength.

The major pressure was the need to excel. If a Jewish boy were to become "a full-blooded warrior" in czarist Russia, he had to

arm himself not with words but with brainpower. When the child
in "The Story of My Dovecot" passes an examination for admission
to secondary school, where the quota for Jews was tight, he turns
into a celebrity in his father's circle: "In the toast the old man
congratulated my parents and said that I had vanquished all my
foes in single combat: I had vanquished the Russian boys with their
fat cheeks, and I had vanquished the sons of our own vulgar parvenus.
So too in ancient times David King of Judah had overcome Goliath,
and just as I had triumphed over Goliath, so too would our people
by the strength of our intellect conquer the foes who had encircled
us and were thirsting for our blood" *(I, 213)*. Among the weapons
of his education languages held a high place. Hebrew lessons and
Talmudic training were a dreary business, but still they influenced
his writing style. Russian schools emphasized what we today call
"the humanities," and Isaac began his study of French, German,
and English in primary school. As an adult he spoke all three well,
French with a native fluency. Violin lessons, however, were a disaster, and here he drew the line against his father's pedagogical
program.

Though his asthma and nervousness probably derived from the
high demands upon him, they did not stifle the child's natural
spontaneity. His sister, though she comments on his sickliness, also
remembers him as a "gentle, affectionate, taciturn, and observant
[child], who would at times explode into unbridled cheerfulness
when he gave free rein to his extraordinary talent for mimicry."[29]
Photographs show a pensive boy, somewhat melancholy, a touch
defiant, with those large watchful eyes which everyone who knew
Babel noticed.

When Isaac was eleven his father enrolled him in the Nicholas I
Commercial School. The choice was probably dictated by the simple
fact that the place was open to Jews. School was a relief: "Life was
hard at home because from morning to night I was compelled to
study many subjects. I relaxed in school." Here he began to break
away from the confinements of home to discover the variety of the
Odessan scene. Gentiles entered his world. Not everyone, he found,
regarded life as a test: some people enjoyed it. "The school was gay,
rowdy, noisy, and multilingual. Sons of foreign merchants, children
of Jewish brokers, Poles from noble families, Old Believers, and
many grown-up billiard players studied there." With his new friends
he explored the attractions of the port and city (perhaps there was

some sexual exploration as well). As roaming Odessa's streets and beaches gave him amplitude for physical self-expression, in school he encountered an intellectual tradition quite different from solemn biblical study or the legalistic rationalism of the Talmud. A teacher blessed with literary taste introduced him to French literature and the French colony of Odessa. At the age of fifteen Isaac Babel made an odd choice for a Jewish boy in an Ukrainian city of the Russian Empire—he initiated his literary career by writing stories in French![30] Though his love of French literature was genuine, writing in French may have been a way for a growing adolescent to separate himself from the culture into which he was born. It was a fateful decision. Babel had taken his first step into the mainstream of European literature, bypassing the lively but provincial springs of Yiddish literature.

In the World

The *numerus clausus* (quota for Jews) kept Babel out of the University of Odessa, the logical choice for a young man of talent interested in literature. Instead in 1911 he enrolled in the Institute of Finance and Business Studies in Kiev from which he received a degree (the school had moved to Saratov at the outbreak of World War I).

In Kiev Babel was introduced into the home of Boris Gronfein, a prosperous business acquaintance of his father's, where he met his future wife Evgeniya (colloquially Zhenya). Gronfein opposed the marriage of his daughter to the impecunious student, and in 1919 they eloped. The Gronfeins had advanced even further along the road to cultural assimilation than the Babels. Music, art, and literature formed part of the fabric of family life. Evgeniya, who was just as independent as her husband-to-be, was planning a career as an artist and immersed herself in books and paintings. Nathalie says of her parents that "from adolescence on [they] shared a commitment to art and a belief that one ought to sacrifice everything for it."[31] As the traditional Jewish (and Russian) community disintegrated under the impact of secularization, some sought a home in millenial socialism, others in nationalism, the Babels in art.

"My parents were determined to live heroically," Nathalie continues. "My mother refused to wear the furs and pretty dresses her parents gave her. My father, to harden himself, would walk bareheaded in the dead of winter without an overcoat, dressed only in a jacket."[32] Years later, at the height of the purges, Mandelstam asked Babel why he spent his evenings with murderous agents of the secret police: "Was it a desire to see what it was like in the exclusive store where the merchandise was death? Did he just want to touch it with his fingers? No, Babel replied, '. . . I just like to have a sniff and see what it smells like.' "[33] He had put behind him the world of his fathers, that world of middle-class Odessan shopkeepers and salesmen struggling for acceptance and respectability, to pursue a life of risk.

The year 1916 found Babel in St. Petersburg (Petrograd, as it was called at the time) out to try his luck as a writer. He had applied for admission to the Law Department of the Petrograd Psychoneurological Institute, but this may have been merely a ploy to gain a residence permit. After suffering rejection from shortsighted editors, he dropped by the office of Maxim Gorky's monthly journal *Letopis* (The chronicle). Gorky, a generous mentor to aspiring writers, befriended him and published two of his early efforts. The stories, "Ilya Isaakovich and Margarita Prokofevna" and "Mama, Rimma, and Alla," got him into difficulties on grounds they were pornographic, though by today's standards the works are quite inoffensive. Several brilliant young writers, among them Viktor Shklovsky and Vladimir Mayakovsky, were associated with *Letopis,* and Babel made their acquaintance. He also worked briefly for a Petrograd newspaper, *Zhurnal zhurnalov* (Journal of journals). The young man had entered the world of letters.

Babel was not one to idealize people, but his regard for Gorky (the man, not the writer) approached veneration, even when we allow for the practical advantages of praising that nabob of Soviet literature in print. All his life Babel remained deeply grateful for the fatherly interest the famous writer took in his career. Their first encounter, as Babel described it, was one between a callow, soft, as yet unshaped youth, and an older man steeled by the school of hard knocks. Gorky's "size, leanness, the power and breadth of his frame, the blue of his small and unflinching eyes" struck the young man, who remembered himself as "a rosy, plump, unfermented mixture of Tolstoyan and Social Democrat." Gorky taught lessons of strength, not accommodation. He had for many years tramped around Russia, struggling to survive on odd jobs, living at the bottom. Gorky was the quintessential self-made man who views life as a battleground where the strong, daring, and courageous win out and the weak fall by the wayside.

The hours he spent in the *Letopis* office, Babel writes, were among the most significant of his life. Gorky had warned him that "a writer's path . . . , is strewn with nails. . . . You will have to walk on them barefoot, a good deal of blood will flow, and with each year it will flow more freely. If you're weak—they'll buy and sell you, harass you to death, lull you to sleep, and you'll fade away while pretending to be a tree in bloom." But the battle is worth it, for there is no higher calling than "constantly to increase, whatever the obstacles, the number of beautiful and necessary things on earth." Seeing that his young charge needed toughening, the older man advised him to "go into the world [*v lyudi*]."[34] Babel probably did not need the advice. He was already on a hunt for experience.

Though he published some stories and sketches immediately before and after the Revolution, Babel regarded the years 1917 to 1923 as his period of initiation into the world: "My assignment *{komandirovka}* lasted seven years. I tramped many roads, was the witness of many battles" *(I, 318)*. Exempted for reasons of health from military service in World War I, he nevertheless signed up in 1917 and served on the Rumanian front, where he caught malaria. During the Revolution he published in another Gorky enterprise, *Novaya zhizn* (New life), where Gorky took a tough anti-Bolshevik line, a fact suppressed in the Soviet Union. Whatever Babel's politics may have been at the time, he participated in their cause. He worked briefly for the notorious Cheka, the first of the Soviet secret police agencies, though most likely his duties were limited to clerical and propaganda work.[35] The summer of 1918 found him in the Volga region as part of an expedition to requisition grain. After his return to revolution-torn Petrograd, he accepted employment with the People's Commissariat of Education (writers were taking bureaucratic positions merely to stay alive). The following year he was in uniform again, with the Reds in the Civil War, fighting as a member of the Northern Army against the White Army of General Yudenich during his attack on Petrograd in October of 1919. He also found time to run off to Odessa to get married.

In 1920 Babel took one of the most consequential steps of his young life. He joined Field Marshal Semyon Budyonny's First Cavalry Army, which was engaged in driving the Poles out of the Ukraine, Byelorussia, and Lithuania. Poland, taking advantage of the confused situation created by the Civil War, had intervened to assert old territorial claims. The Russian armies were initially successful but were routed in a dramatic turnabout as they approached Warsaw. Budyonny's army was composed largely of Cossacks. For centuries the notoriously anti-Semitic Cossacks of the Ukraine had struck fear into the hearts of Jews. Though the Revolution was blurring traditional roles, a Jewish Cossack at one time would have been as bizarre as a black Klu Klux Klansman. True, Babel was attached to the First Cavalry as a correspondent, but in the chaos of Revolution and Civil War the distinction between civilian and soldier was not finely drawn, and he did see action. His diary entries show he was already planning to turn what he had seen and felt into a book.[36] He returned to Odessa exhausted, covered with vermin, and suffering from an acute attack of asthma, and with his fill of experience.

Babel spent the next few years in the south of Russia, living near Odessa in a dacha overlooking the sea, traveling to the Caucasus for relief from his chronic asthma and the seclusion he needed for creative work. He dated the true beginnings of his literary career to these post-Revolutionary years: "Only in 1923 did I learn to express my thoughts clearly and not to excessive length" (*I, 24*). His southern sojourn saw the virtual completion (from the summer of 1921 through the spring of 1923) of a cycle of four stories entitled *Odessa Tales* and centering on the colorful Jewish gangsters of the Moldavanka ghetto. Ever on the lookout for exotic scenes and social renegades, Babel had briefly lived among these mobsters. The first story of *Red Cavalry* appeared in February of 1923. In the summer at his mountain retreat near Batum he began intensive work on the remainder, and finished two years later, in Moscow. Through April of 1925 individual stories appeared in scattered newspapers and magazines and the entire work came out in book form the following year.[37] Since literature could not yet furnish him a livelihood, Babel had worked for a while in a government printing house in Odessa and as a journalist for a Tiflis newspaper, *Zarya vostoka* (Dawn of the east).

Red Cavalry (and, to a lesser extent, *Odessa Tales*) made Babel a Soviet celebrity. "Soviet writer" is a term so discredited by Stalinist duplicity that it becomes difficult to recapture what it meant in the 1920s. The Leninist coup d'état of October 1917 had instituted a dictatorship of the Communist party. Individual rights, never ex-

tensively recognized in Russia, were narrowly restricted. Nevertheless, the destruction of civil society and the attempted mobilization
of every institution and individual in the service of a totalitarian
state still lay in the future and was scarcely imaginable, even to the
mind of a Stalin. In the twenties one could not openly oppose
Bolshevik rule, but history is replete with epochs—Augustan Rome,
the France of Louis XIV—when the absence of political freedom
did not noticeably impede cultural creativity. Though political pressures on artists were intense and ominous, culture in the first decade
of Communist rule still maintained preserves of autonomy. Style
was free, private life was still a legitimate subject, topics were
proscribed but not yet prescribed, at least not by force, intellectual
arguments were wide-ranging and intense. Cultural pluralism par-
alleled the economic pluralism of Lenin's New Economic Policy,
which permitted a limited private market to win the cooperation
of the peasants and to restore the economy from the devastation of
the Civil War and the indiscriminate nationalization of the early
years of Bolshevik rule. Militant Communists shrilly denounced the
ideologically uncommitted, but the Party, though the final arbiter,
kept a neutral if watchful eye on matters not directly impinging on
politics. In the twenties idealistic men and women could still believe
that injustices and betrayals of principle were merely the birth pains
of a new world in the making.

For many of his contemporaries Babel embodied the promise of
Soviet literature. He had participated in the great events of the Civil
War, which was already acquiring mythical status; he was not, like
Gorky, Blok, or Mayakovsky, known before 1917; and he had
produced a masterpiece about the formative experience of the new
society, an epos of the Russian Revolution. As early as 1921 Babel
was the object of hero worship in his native Odessa, which a contemporary explained by his position as "our first authentic Soviet
writer." When the *Red Cavalry* stories appeared another fellow writer
noted, "Babel is creating an uproar in Moscow. . . . Everyone is
ecstatic about him."[38]

In 1924 Babel took his family north to Moscow. If he looked
forward to enjoying the life of a literary lion in the capital he was
in for some rude shocks. The literary politics of the time were
wearying. He was compelled to make changes in the manuscript of
Red Cavalry to eliminate "dangerous spots." General Budyonny, in
an article whose title is a pun maligning Babel's manliness, *"Babizm*

Babelya" (Babel's womanishness), accused him of failing to show
the revolutionary élan of the Cossacks. *Pravda,* the official organ of
the Communist party, while praising his artistic powers and calling
him "a rising star of our literature," cautioned him against the
"dangerous deviations of naturalism and eroticism," a frequent complaint of puritanical Communists about his work. In November
1924 Budyonny as plaintiff and Babel as defendant were invited
to argue their cases at a public meeting, but neither showed up. In
the course of the vigorous debate the Party line was reiterated: Babel
is talented, but he fails to depict the Red Army with sufficient
heroic glamor or show the leading role of the Communist party,
and besides he is too difficult for "ordinary" workers and peasants.
The battle flared up again in 1928. Gorky came to Babel's defense,
and Budyonny counterattacked. At Gorky's prompting Stalin called
a temporary truce with the categorical pronouncement: *"Red Cavalry*
is not so bad as all that; in fact, it's a very good book" *(I,* 435).[39]

     In the following decade such public denunciations by official
organs would indicate that a man's fate was sealed. In the twenties
the future of Soviet culture still seemed an open issue, and the more
independent minded fought back. In May of 1924 Babel and thirty-
five other writers signed a letter of protest against the militant On
Guardists, a group calling for an ideologically pure proletarian literature and in whose journal, *Oktyabr* (October), Budyonny's con-
demnation had appeared. The situation, if not yet hopeless, was
depressing: "Like everyone else in my profession, I am oppressed
by the prevailing conditions of our work in Moscow; that is, we
are seething in a sickening professional environment devoid of art
or creative freedom. And now that I am swaggering among the
generals, I feel it more strongly than before."[40]

     The state of public discourse was souring the fruits of success,
and private life was adding its own difficulties. Babel's marriage
was rocky, and in 1925 his wife, hostile to the Soviet regime and
piqued by an affair he was having with an actress, emigrated to
Paris. His sister had been living in Brussels since February and his
mother followed the next year. To his loneliness was added the
strain of supporting three households, in addition to assorted relatives he generously assisted. His nerves were on edge; his asthma
tormented him. "Babel," an acquaintance observed, "plans his life
on the assumption that he has five years to live."[41] Until the mid-
twenties his life had been a young man's search for experience, self-

discovery, and creative expression, culminating in the brilliant success of *Red Cavalry*. In the future it was to be guided by a strategy of survival, a way to hold on in a culture gone mad.

The crunch began in 1928. The Russian Association of Proletarian Writers (RAPP), a militant Communist organization, launched a vitriolic campaign against "fellow travelers," a term coined by Trotsky to describe intellectuals, like Babel, who accepted the Revolution but had not submitted to the discipline and specific aims of the Communist party. The support of the Party gave RAPP great, if briefly enjoyed, power. These were the years of the First Five Year Plan (1928–32), and artists were expected to be soldiers in the battle to construct a socialist society. Writers were dispatched to industrial sites and agricultural collectives to report upon the glories (but not the painful realities) of construction and social engineering. The triumph of Stalin's policy of "Socialism in One Country," which abandoned the Marxist-Leninist dogma that socialism could result only from an international revolution, increasingly isolated the Soviet Union from the community of nations, encouraging nationalistic xenophobia (with an admixture of anti-Semitism), and obsessive preoccupation with loyalty.

On 23 April 1932, the Central Committee of the Communist party issued a historic decree. It abolished *all* literary organizations, including proletarian groups like RAPP, whose aggressive militancy might be difficult to control, replacing them with a single company union, the Union of Soviet Writers. Its first Congress met in 1934, and to this day any writer who wants his work to see the light of day must belong. The Congress prescribed an official style, that of socialist realism. The daring and often brilliant experiments of the Russian avant-garde, among which Babel's work must be numbered, had already petered out, partly because of a waning of its energies, partly under the onslaught of ideologically minded critics and editors. The imposition of "realism" as an obligatory mode sounded its death knell.

The "realism" of socialist realism is not to be understood as the rendering of objective reality, as Andrey Zhdanov, Stalin's spokesman in intellectual matters, made only too clear at the 1934 Congress. It is instead the depiction "of real life in its revolutionary development" that marks the difference between bourgeois realism and the "socialist" variety. The socialist writer must sow the seeds of the future in the soil of the present. He cannot remain content with showing the world as it is; he must also indicate what it ought to be. The heroes of literature are to be "active builders of a new life"; writers, in Stalin's words, are "engineers of human souls."[42] Socialist realism is unabashedly tendentious. Its ideal is not literature but propaganda. Since the Communist party is the final judge in ideological matters, in practice socialist realism has meant whatever the Party at any given moment wants it to mean. In the twenties the Russian writer with a personal vision was, as he had always been, a lonely, embattled figure. In the thirties, if he wanted to survive, he had to become a functionary of the state.

Babel tried to play the game, but without much success. Early in 1928 he wrote of his inability to become a "professional" writer: his inspiration, he thought, was so deeply personal he could not work on demand. By the following year he realized he had no choice: "I want to become the sort of professional writer I have not until now been" (I, 439, 445). He joined the army of writers recruited by the state, and toured the Ukraine and southern Russia in search of material for a novel about collectivization. Though he made a start, he could not bring himself to finish it. Another projected novel would have shown the reform of a reprobate by the new Soviet morality. As a writer Babel was drawn to the past and gripped by the present; the promise of the future was lifelessly abstract. His play *Maria* (1935) has the curious distinction of invoking a paragon of Communist virtue who never once appears on stage!

In June of 1930 Babel took a job as secretary of the village soviet at Molodenovo, some thirty miles from Moscow, where he lived on and off for the next few years. It was a way of demonstrating his participation in the task of building socialism and, perhaps more important, a refuge from the threatening atmosphere of Moscow. Solitude close to nature was bracing. Through the thirties Babel tried to remain inconspicuous.

As writers became de facto employees of the state, they obtained material rewards and privileges. Babel eventually received a comfortable dacha in the the pleasant environs of the writer's colony at Peredelkino, use of an automobile (an eight cylinder Ford) and a chauffeur, and other benefits that made him part of the Soviet elite. In return he was expected not only to toe the line, but to support the regime at public meetings, lectures, and in journalistic hack work. To his credit, his performances were considerably less frequent than was customary and lacked the ideological fervor that was the standard of the time. The paucity of his output in the thirties is evidence enough that his heart was not in it: he merely did what he felt he had to do. He spent much of his energy in dodging his publishers. Film scripts—both his own and those he edited for others—were a source of income.

Despite the difficulties, Babel produced some work of high quality in the late twenties and the thirties: the play *Sunset* (1928); the story "Awakening" (1931), which along with "In the Basement" (1931) rounded out the *Dovecot* cycle; and the splendid stories "Guy de Maupassant" (1932) and "Di Grasso" (1937). The bulk of his corpus—*Red Cavalry,* the *Odessa Tales,* and the first of the childhood stories of the *Dovecot* series—was the outgrowth of a youthful outburst of of creative energy sustained over only five years, from 1921 through 1925. Its major theme, as often in the fiction of the young, is the quest of a child and young man for self-definition. In the Stalinist years Babel's output was spasmodic. He found himself in the position of being damned when he did and damned when he didn't. His occasional publications were met coolly, sometimes with hostility, even when he strained to accommodate. His silence provoked suspicion: "As long as I don't publish I am merely accused of laziness. If, on the other hand, I publish, then a veritable avalanche of weighty and dangerous accusations will descend upon my head. I feel like a beautiful girl at a ball, with whom everyone wishes to dance. If I were to let myself be persuaded, however, the entire gathering, like a single person, would instantly turn against me. . . . To dance at this ball as I do—this is surely a provocative impropriety, a wild and dangerous example!"[43]

At the First Congress of Soviet Writers Babel felt constrained to defend his failure to publish regularly. His speech is a masterpiece of equivocation: "I spoke of respect for the reader. I perhaps suffer from hypertrophy of that feeling. I have such unbounded respect for him that I am struck dumb." Behind the ironic screen of self-deprecation the discerning might detect an assertive note. Proclaiming himself "a master of the genre of silence," he managed to make silence seem a virtue in an age when everybody was speaking "unbearably loudly." Though he did not intend his silence as a political protest—in 1934 such a gesture would have been suicidal—he advocated an aesthetic for the socialist era quite different from the rhetorical bombast and lifeless abstractions of socialist realism. "The style of the Bolshevik epoch lies in manliness, restraint," he held.

It is filled with fire, passion, power, joy" *(I, 408–10)*. The style
he described was very much his own.

Though he published relatively little, in his correspondence of
the thirties Babel often refers to creative projects. The mystery
surrounding their nature and fate has provoked speculation that he
may have been working on material he knew would not meet the
approval of the watchdogs of culture, that he was, as Russians say,
"writing for the desk drawer." But it is more likely that he suc-
cumbed to the very human temptation to deceive himself, believing
that he could somehow reconcile his creative gifts with the requirements of the social order in which he had to live. As late as 1935
he could write: "In a country as united as ours, it is quite inevitable
that a certain amount of thinking in clichés should appear, and I
want to overcome this standardized way of thinking and introduce
into our literature new ideas, new feelings and rhythms" *(I, 283)*.

What was Babel's attitude toward Soviet society? He may or may
not have been the confirmed Leninist a friend of the 1920s thought
him,[44] but he most certainly welcomed the Russian Revolution.
However, he was also too humane not to be disturbed by its brutality, too intelligent not to be aware of the hypocrisies and ine-
quities it spawned. After long bouts with officialdom, he was
permitted to visit his family abroad in 1927 and again in 1932. In
the freedom of Paris he complained bitterly of the betrayal of the
Revolution.[45] He had another chance to defect in 1935 when he
and Boris Pasternak, at the last moment and only at the insistence
of the French, were included in the Russian delegation to an international antifascist meeting in Paris. Yet he returned.

Part of his dilemma was that of the writer generally, for his
creative medium is words. A Chagall or a Stravinsky, with a universal language at his disposal, can find an audience anywhere. For
Babel emigration, however appealing the freedom of the West,
appeared as the deracinated, meaningless existence of a Russian taxi
driver in Paris. He had come to feel he was Russian to the bone:
"Spiritual life has more nobility in Russia. Russia has poisoned me.
I long for her, I think only of her." Returning home from one of
his trips abroad, he wrote, "My native land greeted me with autumn,
poverty and what she alone has for me—poetry." Too much the
Russian to abandon his country, too much a man of words to cut
himself off from its language, he also had a strong sense of historical
destiny. His duty was to art and to history. Life might be easier in

the West, but Russia was where the action was: "To live here [Paris] is an excellent thing as regards individual freedom, but we Russians miss the winds of great thoughts and great passions." Unruly Cossacks, bigoted peasants, sadistic secret police, dim-witted bureaucrats could not blur his vision of the Russian Revolution as a momentous event in human history, a terrible birth whose issue was unclear but whose fate he wished to share. In 1935, on the eve of the great purges, he expressed the desire to see his daughter (whose safety he would not have risked merely to impress the postal censors) grow up "a citizen of a young flourishing country full of sap and vigor, and with a future." He was too clear-headed not to have doubts: in his last years fear was his constant companion. Dark destiny had reduced him to playing a waiting game: "I am incapable of compromise, be it internal or external," he wrote, "and so I have to suffer, retreat inside myself, and wait." If hope at times deserted him, he never lost courage or that ironical poise that grows out of a mature understanding of human foolishness. When all else failed, his powerful sense of duty kept him at what he saw as his post: "There's no going back now," he wrote in 1931. "I must toe the line. . . . the last act of the tragedy or comedy—I don't know which—has started. Don't jog my hand, *mes enfants*. If you only knew how much that hand needs to be firm and steady."[46]

After returning to Russia from the 1935 Congress, Babel gave up on bringing his family home. He remarried and started a second family with Antonina Nikolaevna Pirozhkova, an engineer whom he had met in the early thirties. He fathered a second daughter, Lidiya, in 1937. From 1936 through 1938, when millions of Russians were arrested, many killed, others placed in concentration camps, Babel sought safety in isolation and obscurity. In his letters occasional notes of anxiety break through a thickening screen of reticence. He must have known his days were numbered.

The blow fell on 15 May 1939. At ten o'clock in the morning Babel was arrested at his dacha in Peredelkino and taken to the dreaded Lubyanka prison in Moscow. Much ink has been spilled over the reason for his arrest on the naive assumption that people were not arrested and killed without having done *something*. An NKVD officer who participated in the infamous purges knew better: "People are always trying to explain things by fixed laws. When you've looked behind the scenes as I have you know that blind chance rules a man's life in this country of ours." By the end of

1938, 5 percent of the population, or one in twenty Soviet men and women, had been arrested overall, and the odds against intellectuals were considerably worse. Of the 700 writers who attended the First Writer's Congress of 1934 (all of them then regarded as loyal Soviet citizens, many of them card-carrying Communists) only fifty lived to see the Second Congress of 1954, though 71 percent had not reached the age of forty by the earlier date.[47]

The question that perhaps should be asked is not why Babel was arrested in 1939 but how he survived until then. Babel had done some dangerous things. He had been abroad and maintained contact with foreigners, a flagrant cause of suspicion in this paranoid climate; he bravely opened his home to the relatives of "the vanished"; his silence provoked the ideological hounds. Perhaps the low profile he kept helped. The fact that he was arrested after the tidal wave of the great purges had ebbed suggests that he enjoyed special protection. Gorky, whose world-wide reputation gave him exceptional influence, befriended Babel and numerous other writers until his own death in 1936, probably at the hands of Stalin's agents. For the next two years Nikolay Ezhov, "the blood-thirsty dwarf," lorded it over the most murderous machine in human history (the Nazis had yet to make their bid for first place). Babel, either out of fascination with evil or in hopes of averting the blow, maintained a friendship with Ezhov's wife. But Ezhov disappeared mysteriously in February of 1939, devoured by the same monster he had fed with the lives of millions. Babel was arrested only three months later.

To this day the exact circumstances of Babel's death are uncertain. The death certificate reads 17 March 1941. However, since no one knows of his whereabouts after his arrest, it is quite possible that he was shot immediately in the Lubyanka basement, as were countless others. On 23 December 1954, after Stalin's death, he was officially exonerated of "a crime." Bystanders, who saw him whisked off to Lubyanka report that he was calm, even smiling. His last recorded words were: "They didn't let me finish."[48]

Chapter Two

Literary Trends and Babel's Views of His Craft

Trends

The Revolution of 1917 transfigured Russian society and culture. No writer could ignore an upheaval of such magnitude. The tumultous years of revolution and civil war gave rise to a literature of violent extremes. The unparalleled effort of the victorious Communists to manufacture according to plan a new society and even a new human being challenged traditional assumptions about human nature. The Revolution, it seemed, had opened a breach in history, irrevocably sundering the past from the present. Thinking Russians asked themselves: What, if any, were the moral limits of violence? What was the proper relation of means and ends? Could the past really be scrapped, the memories of several thousand years of Western culture blotted out, and if so, what would be the human consequences of such a radical transformation? Some answered with their feet and fled, creating a Russian culture in exile. Others—the so-called proletarian writers, many of the futurists—responded with affirmation to the Utopian ambitions of the new order. Most of the important Soviet writers of the twenties, Babel included, stood somewhere in the middle—uncertain, anxious, cautiously hopeful. Rapid historical change is a cause for optimism or apprehension. This double tendency is reflected in the literature of the time, which at one extreme tends to the idealizing modes of panegyric and ode or the wishful idyll, and at the other to the anxious gestures of satire and nostalgia. Since superior works of literature embrace wide ranges of feeling, we may encounter both poles in a single work, such as Yury Olesha's *Envy,* a highly original blend of idyllic imaginings and dark satire, or Isaac Babel's *Red Cavalry,* with its mix of irony, nostalgia, and celebration of heroic action. What is generally absent from the literature of the twenties is the calmly objective rendering of social reality we call "realism."

The avoidance of realistic conventions was part of the legacy of Russian symbolism. Symbolism, which dominated the artistic scene in the century's first decade, was born of a widespread sense of historical crisis. For the Russian symbolists history was a nightmare from which they sought deliverance. Modern industrial society, compartmentalized by division of labor and controlled by impersonal bureaucracies, had lost its wholeness; integrated communities had given way to mass man, isolated and lonely. The center no longer held. "The equilibrium between man and nature, life and art, science and music, civilization and culture has been lost," the poet Alexander Blok lamented. "Everything is multiplied; nothing coheres."[1] Finding Western civilization at a dead end, the symbolists sought escape in millenial hopes and metaphysical speculations. In their yearning to transcend history they were a throwback to an earlier generation of European, especially German, romanticism. Except for a few aesthetes, the Russian symbolists were Neoplatonists, seeking an ultimate Oneness behind the fragmented shards of contemporary life, the permanence of a transcendental Absolute to counter the meaningless flux of the phenomenal world. The things around us, they proclaimed, are confinements of the spirit, of value only insofar as they "correspond" to a higher order of reality. We live in "a forest of symbols," they said, citing Baudelaire's famous sonnet "Correspondences." "Everything transitory is merely an image," they repeated after Goethe's *Faust*.

However, if the symbolists' thought echoed the nineteenth-century search for ideological totality, their literary practice was radically innovative. Symbolism looked at the world with the head of Janus, one face turned back to the century of ideologies, the other forward to the modernist movements of the coming century. They regarded the exhaustive, meticulously detailed novels of realism as anachronistic in an age of turmoil and social dislocation. The world was moving too fast for the leisurely investigations of society indulged in by a Tolstoy or a Goncharov. If reality was essentially chaos, there was little point in the analytic procedure of the psychological novel, which could only peel away the layers of the mind as if it were an onion, never to arrive at its transcendental essence.

The queen of the arts for the symbolists was music, which they regarded as "pure," uncluttered by the dull matter of this world. Of the literary arts, the lyric poem comes closest to music. The lyric impulse so dominated the symbolist imagination that even their occasional novels, short stories, and plays are lyrical. The symbolist movement breathed new life into Russian poetry, which since Pushkin's time had been overshadowed by the realistic novel and abused by critics and readers using literature for political purposes. It inaugurated the Silver Age of Russian literature, of which the avant-garde of the twenties wrote the final episode. The Golden Age is that of Pushkin, but if we exclude that singular genius, silver must rate as more precious than gold. From the 1890s through the early 1920s more poets of the first rank came to prominence than in any comparable period of Russian history.

The symbolist lyric was a poem of shadowy nuances. Since the ordinary world had value only as it intimated other, truer worlds, the symbolist poet suggested and did not tell, evoked rather than described. Turning his back on the mimetic aspirations of realism, he placed the medium of literature, language, at the forefront of his concern. Language was clothed in mysterious drapes; writing became a "process of conjuring" where "every word is a magical formula." The poem was an incantation designed to capture "a magically experienced reality."[2] Metaphor, which links one class of things to another and therefore could, it was thought, leap from the finite to the infinite, replaced the exact fitting of the word to object sought by realism. Myth supplanted its models of objective social reality. To create his evocations of otherworldly realms the symbolist poet employed loose and flowing rhythms, words with ethereal overtones in strange combinations. He wove an airy fabric of sounds that would seem, in Verlaine's phrase, "plus vague et soluble dans l'air" (vague and soluble in air).

The avant-garde groups of the years after 1910—the futurists and acmeists as well as a substantial segment of the first generation of Soviet writers—defined themselves in opposition to symbolism. Though the arguments were complex, the great divide ran between a view of the artist as seer and a view of the artist as craftsman (or, among the futurists, as technician). For the postsymbolist generation words were "things," not magical formulae; works of art were "made," not intuited; the artist used "devices," not prophetic inspiration. Spurning the metaphysical quests of symbolism, its "hopeless Germanic earnestness," the acmeists put in a claim for irony, wit, and clarity, models of which they discovered (as did Babel) in French literature. The futurists, repelled by the "sweetness and melodiousness" of the symbolist style, worked for a "tougher," more "pro-

saic" manner.[3] Another prewar group, the *Zavety* (Legacy), led by
Aleksey Remizov, had a large and as yet insufficiently appreciated
impact upon Soviet writers of the early twenties (one of its members
was the influential Evgeny Zamyatin). The *Zavety* writers regarded
the symbolist dream of a universal language of symbol and myth
as eclectic, Alexandrian, and un-Russian. They set out to de-latinize
and de-Frenchify the Russian literary language, to instill in it the
vigor and raciness of colloquial speech and folk traditions. These
several tendencies came to a head in the first years of Soviet literature
as writers sought to substitute vividness for hazy mystery, irony for
portentousness, a tough Russianized language for the international
style of symbolism.

But when children rebel against their fathers they do not cease
to resemble them. Though they rejected the mystical aspirations of
symbolism, the writers of the avant-garde were still indebted to its
formal innovations and continued to value language for its aesthetic
powers instead of regarding it as a system of neutral signs. Much
of early Soviet prose is lyrical; myth and metaphor play a large role.
Of the symbolist writers the figure of Andrey Bely, the master of
"ornamental prose," looms large on the horizon of the twenties.
Especially in his remarkable novel *St. Petersburg* (1916), Bely is more
a demolisher of received traditions than a creater of new mythologies.
The verve of his prose, its complex rhythms and startling combinations, seemed to his followers to catch the quick pulse of modern
life. His corrosive parodies and ironies, including a reflexive irony
that implicates the work itself and makes the position it adopts
toward its reader highly ambiguous, appealed to a generation that
liked to see itself as tough-minded. Among the many contributions
of symbolism was a widening of the limits of the permissible in
literature. An interest in the irrational aspects of experience and
imagination, in dream, in the darker sides of sexuality and aggression, in grotesquerie, survives into the twenties.

Indeed, so pervasive was the influence of symbolism that Zamyatin, a brilliant critic as well as an outstanding writer, described
early Soviet prose as a synthesis of symbolism and realism. The
demands of life in a revolutionary era, Zamyatin argued, were too
insistent to allow the artist to ignore reality. Yet in abandoning the
metaphysical flights of symbolism and returning to the conflicts
and struggles of contemporary reality, the first generation of Soviet
writers could not free itself from the formal strategies of symbolism.

The new writing might be viewed as a manifestation of symbolist aesthetics minus symbolist ideology. What had taken the place of ideology (except for those who found a home in Marxism) was ironic skepticism.[4]

Such a position is profoundly problematical. Symbolism, whatever its shortcomings, attempted to forge a coherent philosophy of life. In scuttling metaphysics the modernists found themselves without a shared belief. One way out of the postsymbolist dilemma was to proclaim form a self-sufficient value, to identify art with craft or technique. The outstanding critical school of the period, whose members proudly assumed the name "formalists," did just that.

Babel's Views

Babel shared the postsymbolist view of art as craft. "Don't talk to me about creative work à la Mozart, about the blissful time spent over a manuscript, about the free flow of the imagination!" he told his fellow writer Konstantin Paustovsky. Though in his fiction Babel often asserts the powers of imagination, in speaking about art he insists upon the painstaking labor it demands: "When I'm writing the shortest story, I still have to work at it as if I were required to dig up Mount Everest all by myself with a pick and shovel. . . . I work like a mule, but I'm not complaining. I chose this forced labor myself. I'm like a galley slave, chained for life to his oar and in love with it, with every detail of it, with the very wood polished by his hands. After years of contact with human skin the roughest wood takes on a fine color and becomes like ebony. It's just the same with our words, with the Russian language. You have only to put your warm hand to it and it becomes a living precious thing." As the creative process is not one of magical inspiration, the value of its products does not lie in a special wisdom. Literature may treat the most ordinary of experiences. Not content, he held, but style turns the trick: "It's style that does it, it's style that does it. I can write a short story about washing underwear and it will read like Julius Caesar's prose. It's a matter of language and style."[5]

Though art is a kind of craftsmanship, it is not quite the same as making a chair or repairing a dishwasher. Babel spurns the symbolist (and romantic) identification of creativity with the faculty of imagination, but he follows his predecessors in their high estimation of the writer's calling. In their revolt against the symbolist-romantic heritage, the post-1910 modernists retained its heroic image of the artist. The artist in Paustovsky's memoirs of Babel appears as a kind of martyr-saint, "chained for life to his oar" and yet in love with his servitude.

The aim of this Flaubertian dedication is to impart life to matter. The form, Babel implies, is already latent in the material. The function of craft is to make it visible (sculptors speak of their art this way). Human hands working at the roughest wood bring out its latent sheen. In the same way the writer, who has his warm hand on the pulse of the Russian language, brings out the beauties hidden in it. "A phrase is born into the world," Babel writes else-where, "both good and bad at the same time. The secret consists in a twist, barely perceptible. The lever must lie in the hand and grow warm, and you may turn it only once, not twice." (I, 273).

Actually Babel turned the lever many times: his six-page story "Lyubka the Cossack" went through twenty-two versions totalling some two hundred pages! But the point is the same. Art is not a construction from nothing. It shapes potentialities, material with given natures. These natures are morally and aesthetically neutral— they may be "good" or "bad," ugly or beautiful. If the lever is turned correctly, they are purified of their dross and appear as unequivocally beautiful, and also "living." The final product of the work of art is an analogue of a living organism. An artist must respect the nature of things so that he may raise them to a higher plane of nature. "A man who doesn't live in nature," Babel writes in one of his stories, "as a stone does or an animal, will never in all his life write two worthwhile lines" (I, 260). Art, one cannot help feeling, was a way for this Jewish boy of the city to touch nature, to put his warm hand to the rough wood and make it lovely.

Style and form, then, are not mere adornments of ideas, but rather the essence of art. The creative act is its own justification. Its value does not lie in what it may teach but in the very process by which experienced objects are shaped into beautiful forms, in-different language into a beautiful style. This is not to say that Babel was an apostle of the hedonistic aestheticism of "art for art's sake" so fashionable at the turn of the century but by then obsolete. Though the artist's virtue lies not in what he says but how he says it, it is nevertheless a moral virtue. Through the act of art, which gives form to the raw stuff of nature and language, the artist dem-onstrates his truthfulness, integrity, and courage. Art is neither a mirror of experience as it was for classicism and realism, nor the romantic-symbolist passage from experience to the transcendental. For Babel, as James Falen has astutely noted, art *is* experience, a way for the soul to participate in the world.[6]

My motto is *authenticity*. . . . What I do is to get hold of some trifle, some little anecdote, a piece of market gossip, and turn it into something I cannot tear myself away from. It's alive, it plays. It's round like a pebble on the seashore. It's held together by the fusion of separate parts, and this fusion is so strong that even lightning can't split it. And people will read the story, they'll remember it, they'll laugh, not because it's funny but because one always feels like laughing in the presence of human good fortune. . . . a demon or angel . . . has taken possession of me, the son of a petty merchant. And I obey him like a slave, like a beast of burden. I have sold my soul to him, and I must write in the best possible way. I guess it's an affliction. But if you take it away from me—either my good fortune or my affliction—the blood will gush out of my veins and my heart along with it; I will be worth no more than a chewed cigarette butt. It's this work that makes me into a man, and not an Odessa street-corner philosopher.[7]

For Babel there can be no "depressing" works of art, an adjective people use to describe novels and films treating subjects they would rather not hear about. To produce a work of art is like giving birth to a child. It is a stroke of "good fortune," which can only add to the world's meager store of happiness. The joy of art lies not in the "uplift" of its message but in the very act of mastering form, of creating life out of matter. Form is not mechanical combination but an organic "fusion of separate parts" so powerfully necessary that "it's alive, it plays." Though the total commitment creation demands may be felt as an "affliction," it gives dignity to life. His work turns Babel into a man, not "an Odessa street-corner philosopher." Odessa street-corner philosophers merely talked about things; they did not make them.

Until the mid-twenties, when the novel revived, the lyric and short story dominated the Soviet scene, as it had the Russia of the prewar era. The chaotic years of revolution and civil war confirmed the sense of writers that only the shorter forms, more receptive to impressionistic imagery and momentary feeling, could do justice to the quickened tempo and violent temper of the times. (Severe paper shortages did not encourage prospective novelists either.) In the above citation Babel describes the short story as a trivial ancecdote brought to life through art; elsewhere he employs Goethe's definition, "the account of an unusual incident." Whether his subjects are drawn from common life or not, the result is almost always striking. An heir of the ornamental school of Andrey Bely and its great teacher, Nikolay Gogol, Babel works with rich colors, paradoxical contrasts ("the fusion of separate parts"), brutal actions, surprising twists, troubling ironies. Fascinated with violence, he does violence to the blank page. His stories may not always be, as he claimed, the result of the most interesting five minutes he has experienced,[8] but they are intended to be something like that for us.

Chapter Three
Early Writings (1913–22)

Babel's originality did not emerge all at once. His first works are naturalistic genre sketches drawn from his experiences of Jewish life in Odessa and southern Russia and his life in Petrograd. "Stary Shloyme" (Old Shloyme, 1913), written while he was still in business school in Kiev, is a study of an old man reduced to an animal existence. When threatened with eviction from the home where he has spent his unhappy life, Shloyme comes alive for a brief moment before committing suicide. The central character is carefully observed but, as often with novice writers, the tale is sentimental and overemphatic. Its theme is the persistent hold of the past. Shloyme considered himself an atheist, but, horrified by his son's intention to convert, he feels how "an old forgotten faith flamed up in him. . . . To leave, completely and forever, his God, the God of a humiliated and suffering people—that he couldn't understand."[1]

The alienation of youth from age is central to an incomplete autobiographical sketch of 1915, "Detstvo u babushki" (Childhood at grandmother's). In grandmother's home, claustrophobic and joyless, barren of the supports of faith or culture, megalomaniacal ambition has supplanted traditional Jewish values. "Study," grandmother tells the child, "study and you will get everything—wealth and glory. You must know everything. Everyone will fall to their knees and grovel before you. Everyone will envy you. Don't trust people. Don't have friends. Don't give them money. Don't give them your heart." The suffocating boy dreams of escaping to the pleasures (sexual among others) that lie outside grandmother's stifling domain. Her tale of his dead grandfather suggests that it is possible to build a life on a principle other than outdoing one's neighbors. Grandfather was a failure, an artist manqué, who yet was possessed of "an inextinguishable thirst for knowledge and life." Such passionate Jews often appear in Babel's fiction as alternatives to the obsessively ambitious petit-bourgeoisie scrambling to escape from the ghetto and the past. The style of the sketch is pedestrian, though its terseness anticipates the mature Babel, as so does the meditative

role of the first-person narrator, who filters past observation through
present consciousness. This strategy permits Babel to add an elegiac
strain to the recitation of mere fact: "The darkening room, grandmother's yellow eyes, her shawl-wrapped figure huddled and silent
in the corner, the warm air, the closed door, the crack of a whip,
its shrill whistle—only now do I understand how strange it was,
how much it portended."[2]

The two stories Babel published in Gorky's *Letopis* in 1916 are
also written in a naturalistic vein. "Mama, Rimma, and Alla" describes
the goings-on in a Moscow boardinghouse, again involving a generational conflict. Tightfisted Mama worries about money while her
daughters, thirsting for independence, explore sex. Alla gets into
trouble, Rimma performs an abortion in the bathroom, the story ends
with a letter from Mama to her husband imploring him to return
home and exert masculine authority. The language is as flat as the
milieu (gentile, though still lower middle class) is squalid. The
colloquial dialogue of a Jewish traveling salesman and a local prostitute (in Orel) give "Ilya Isaakovich and Margarita Prokofevna"
more vitality. Babel would become a master mimic of uneducated
speech. Despite the gulf separating Jewish businessman from Russian whore, they still manage to reach each other. Though tinged
by sentimentality, the duo of this chance encounter are convincingly
human.[3]

Journalism can provide excellent training in brevity and careful
observation. Reportage was one of the routes by which Soviet writers
of the twenties broke away from the esoteric symbolist manner.
Even in his mature fiction Babel often adopts the stance of the
dispassionate reporter recounting the events of the day. The four
sketches he wrote in 1916–17 for the Petrograd daily *Zhurnal zhurnalov* under the heading *Moi listki* (Leaves from my notebook) reflect
an age when newspapers were a source of entertainment as well as
information. They are the casual observations of a walker in the
city, what the French call *feuilletons*. The charm of the form hinges
on the ironic distance separating the author from his subject, a
position Babel was to maintain throughout his career. "Publichnaya
biblioteka" (The public library), a sketch of its personnel and clients,
makes a nod to Gogol, the Russian master of the genre. Like Gogol,
Babel keeps his eye on the eccentric. Members of the library staff
"stand out by virtue of a pronounced physical defect—one has his
fingers all curled up, another's head has dropped to the side and

got stuck there. . . . Gogol would have described them well."
And again, like Gogol, Babel shifts gears from naturalistic detail
to a lyrical coda: "Evening. The reading room is half dark. . . .
Soft snow weaves its weft behind the wide windows. Nearby, on
the Nevsky, life teems. Far away—in the Carpathians—blood flows."
Real life is elsewhere, far from the frustrated dreamers of the library,
their noses jammed into books. "Devyat" (The nine) is similar—a
sketch of nine writers, long on hope but short on talent or luck,
come to an editor's office. Here Babel employs a kind of shorthand
for ironic effect, a technique he returned to in his mature work:
"His name is Sardarov. Profession—satirist. Request—to publish
his satires. He has a foreword by a famous poet. If necessary he can
throw in an afterword." "Odessa" celebrates that city of the sun.
"Vdokhnovenie" (Inspiration), more story than sketch, shows greater
maturity. It consists of a dialogue between the narrator and his
friend Mishka. Mishka has inspiration but little of talent or discipline. As in many of his later stories Babel allows his character to
damn himself in his own words. The narrator's summation throws
an elegiac shadow over the tale, a characteristic Babelian reflection
upon the sadness of things.[4]

Before accepting employment with Gorky's *Novaya zhizn,* Babel
published a sketch, "Doudou," apparently based on his experiences
in World War I, whose narrative economy would make it fit well
with the stories of *Red Cavalry.* Doudou is a French cabaret chanteuse
hurled by the accidents of war into an army hospital. A child of
pity, she offers her breasts to a French aviator with shattered legs.
Fired from her job, she is unrepentant. "I swear to you, . . . I
swear to you that if Diba [a filthy lout] were to ask, I would do
the same," are her concluding words. Babel likes to end powerfully.
People who break the rules to give vent to their natural impulses
continually attract him.[5]

The *Novaya zhizn* sketches are grim. The spring of 1918 was not
a time for the light banter of *feuilletons.* War and revolution had
left their terrible wounds, the economy was in shambles, famine
was widespread. Most of Babel's contributions offer glimpses of
suffering Petrograd; some are muckraking pieces exposing official
corruption and the inability of government agencies to meet the
needs of ordinary people. Though they perhaps embody some apprehension over the course of the Revolution, they are not politically
inspired, for Communist regimes have no monopoly on dishonest

bureaucrats and an uncaring citizenry. Babel's greatest indignation is roused by the plight of suffering children. The real revolution, he writes, is one in which children are cared for properly—a sentiment he would repeat thirteen years later in his tale "Karl-Yankel."[6] In *Novaya zhizn* Babel begins to work out his characteristic style. Terse clauses are reserved for a single perception, modifiers are vivid, metaphors (or similes) are striking. Units of language turn into miniatures as enclosing symmetries set them off from the body of the text. It is a highly dramatized prose, as we may see from the following description of starving animals in a zoo: "The parrots, caught up in a wearisome terror, screech with intolerable scorn. They rub their silvery tongues against the wire. Their curved talons dig into the cage; gray beaks, so similar to tin flutes, open and close, as in a bird dying from thirst. The roseate bodies of the parrots rock rhythmically by the walls." Babel seeks out the extremes of experience. At times he adopts a reportorial coolness, ironic and detached, that makes the horrors he describes stand out in relief: "They were lying side by side in the morgue. Twenty-five corpses— fifteen of them children. All the names were just right for this kind of dreary disaster: Kuzmin, Kulikov, Ivanov. . . . All day long, women . . . crowded between the white coffins. Their faces were just as gray as those of the drowned." His prose can also be mysteriously evocative: "the congregation is standing with lighted candles. The small yellow flames flicker with their breathing. . . . The priests walk about in gleaming mitres. . . . Christ seems to be stretched out in the dark blue of a starry sky."[7]

If Babel's style isolates perceptions, his narrative juxtaposes isolated events. The sketch "Vecher" (Evening) is typical. Like many of Babel's stories it has two scenes and a concluding coda, with the whole tied together by the the mediating consciousness of the nar- rator. Scene 1 describes a young boy shot trying to escape "commissars" (presumably of the Cheka), who overtake him and beat him savagely before the eyes of the horrified narrator, an idle stroller in the city. Scene 2 is of bawdy Petrograd night life—music, glitter, gaiety. The sketch concludes in brooding tones: "The incorporeal veil of night wound about the golden spires. The hushed void concealed a thought—fragile and pitiless." The tale opens with a proclamation—"I won't draw conclusions"—and ends with an inconclusive conclusion, a "thought" that remains unspoken.[8] It is Babel's way to highlight incongruities—violence and suffering, compassion and indifference, cruelty and carefree abandon—and then resolve his story in a reflection of the unfathomable mystery of the world.

"Shabos-Nakhamu," published in another newspaper in 1918, switches to a Jewish milieu and a comic style. The hero is Hershele of Ostropol, a figure of Yiddish folklore, a ne'er-do-well burdened by a shrewish wife and bawling children, who manages to gain by cunning what society will not give for honest labor. In Babel's hands he is more rogue than schlemiel. Pretending to be the incarnation of *Shabos-Nakhamu* (a Jewish holiday), he swindles the landlady of a tavern and her equally dimwitted husband. In his mock-heroic treatment of Hershele Babel again looks back to Gogol: "That's the way things are for every Jew. But Hershele isn't every Jew. His fame had spread to all Ostropol, all Berdichev, all Vilyuysk." Hershele is a Jew rich only in words, and thus a kindred spirit of his author: " 'What did you earn?' his wife asked. 'I earned life everlasting,' he said. 'Both the rich and the poor promised it to me.' '. . . For every other wife a husband is a husband. Mine can only feed his wife on words. May God take away his tongue by the New Year, and his arms and legs too.' 'Amen,' Hershele replied." This folksy aphoristic manner of Yiddish literature, along with cadenced repetitions, spreads to the narrative, creating the illusion of oral improvisation. Extravagant comparisons do much to establish the comic tone: "His wife hurled reproaches. Each was as heavy as a cobblestone. Hershele answered in verse" *(I,* 195–200).[9]

In 1920, shortly before joining Budyonny's cavalry, Babel adapted several anecdotes from a French captain's account of the Great War. Though of no literary merit, Gaston Vidal's potboiler may have reminded him of his experience on the Rumanian front. It also gave him many instances of the grisly brutality to be found in his own war tales. In "Na pole chesti" (On the field of honor) a cowardly soldier is caught masturbating in a ditch; his commanding officer, to shame him into joining the battle, urinates on him; it works, and the poor fellow, charging in despair across an open field, is immediately gunned down. The irony in the title is Babel's. In "Dezertir" (The deserter) a captain, "a splendid fellow and something of a philosopher," gives a frightened boy who has run from battle a chance to salvage his honor by shooting himself. The boy cannot go through with it, and the captain obliges. The shock of "Semeystvo papashi Maresko" (Old Marescot's family) reminds us

of Maupassant's more lurid moments—Marescot's family, we learn
at the end, is in the sack he carries on his shoulders: His wife and
two daughters had been blown up in a bombardment. "Kvaker"
(The Quaker), though published with the other stories, does not
have a source in Vidal's book. The Quaker is a puritanical, pious
man who adores animals and cannot abide people. The stable boy
Baker, a lover of women who cannot stand animals, is his foil.
Disregarding all danger, the Quaker sets out to forage for his animals
and dies "on account of his love for a horse." The story is a coolly
clinical study. The contrast of sensual and cerebral man is a favorite
of Babel's. [10]

Babel worked at language like a loving gardener, pruning away
overgrowth and weeds to get at the essential beauty of the plant.
Perhaps it was this passion for cutting that drove him to rework
Vidal's verbosities (in the thirties, frustrated in his own creative
efforts, he took pleasure in editing the efforts of others). For some
140 words of overblown prose at the start of "The Deserter"—"In
battle he is a raging lion; at rest, a brooding eagle," etc.—he
substituted two terse sentences, in the process converting bombast
into irony: "Captain Génier was a splendid fellow, and something
of a philosopher as well. On the field of battle he would stop at
nothing, but in private life he didn't take offense at small things."
(In an afterword Babel comments drily about the "heroic" captain
who shoots a frightened boy: "That's something, if a man doesn't
take offense at small things.")[11]

Some examples of Babel's journalistic work for the army newspaper *Krasny kavalerist* (The red cavalry man) during his tenure with
the First Cavalry Army have been reprinted. For readers who think
the violence of Babel's war stories is exaggerated, it may be helpful
to learn that one of his reportorial accounts of torture (by the Poles,
of course) is more gruesome than anything to be found in his imaginative literature. The writing in these sketches is often as strong
as in similar things in *Red Cavalry*, but an occasional puffy panegyric
to the heroes of the Red Army would be out of place in that
uncompromising work of art. [12]

The articles Babel wrote in 1922 for the Tbilisi newspaper *Zarya
vostoka* appeared under the pseudonym K. Lyutov (*lyuty* means
"fierce")—he had used the name Kirill Vasilevich Lyutov to dis-
guise his Jewish identity while serving with the Cossacks, and
reverted to it for the major character of *Red Cavalry*. They are not

very interesting. The language is often strained; accounts of literacy campaigns and economic improvements in the Georgian republic do not make for exciting reading.[13] No doubt the restraints upon journalism imposed by a now entrenched Bolshevik power inhibited him.

"Vecher u imperatritsy" (Evening at the empress's), published in the same year, is more rewarding. It is a lush evocation of the Anichkov Palace in St. Petersburg and the family of the last Russian czar. Here Babel plays with decadent mannerisms—"withered flowers crumbling to dust"—overlaid with his ever-present irony.[14]

Chapter Four
Odessa Tales

Within the Russian tradition the playfulness and verbal exuberance of *Odessa Tales* echo Gogol, especially his early Ukrainian stories. Both authors take as their point of departure the genre sketch, which they transform into something highly original. They guide us on excursions to cultural backwaters—Gogol's rustic Dikanka and Mirgorod, Babel's urban ghetto of Moldavanka—where we view the curious locals through tinted glasses. Ordinary life becomes picturesque. Babel's shopkeepers, brokers, whores, and gangsters, like Gogol's country bumpkins, are clothed not in realism's drab dress but in the variegated garments of romance or the crazy quilts of comedy.

Babel's strategies are self-consciously literary. We are made aware that what we are reading is artful, that we are to be amused, not moved. Unlike *Red Cavalry* and the *Dovecot* cycle, *Odessa Tales* is less the product of the personal pressure of experience than of artistic calculation. The tales realize the aesthetic program Babel outlined in his essay "Odessa": to bring Russian literature from somber metaphysical shadows into the clear light of the joyous sun. Here is the way Babel thought he wanted to write, not yet the way he felt he had to write.

Gogol is funnier but Babel is more consistent in his comic attitude. He has no interest in Gogol's gothic horrors or his flights into sublimity. When the language of *Odessa Tales* turns extravagant we can be fairly certain that the author has an ironic tongue firmly planted in his cheek. Both authors establish a complicity of superiority with their readers, the precondition of comedy. Were their characters more complex, they would be less humorous. The Ukrainian and the Moldavanka tales are also related to the travel sketch— they are journeys downward to the lower orders rather than away to distant lands—and the travel sketch characteristically views its subjects from a distance. We read these texts as visitors from respectable society observing people who are quaint, odd, disreputable, but who—and here the irony turns against the reader—possess virtues our straightlaced ways deny us.

In the modern Jewish tradition, which tends toward moral urgency and sentimental pathos, *Odessa Tales* might be regarded as blasphemy. It celebrates sensual life, romanticizes common criminals, and scorns Jewish pieties (and middle-class respectability). It is very much a young man's work.

If Gogol left his mark on Babel's first cycle, so did Nikolay Leskov, that other great master of simulated oral narration or *skaz*. The narrator's pose is that of the raconteur, the teller of tall tales, the spinner of yarns. He makes his presence felt by intruding into the narration or by adopting mannerisms of spoken language (questions, exclamations, sundry colloquialisms): "And now having told the story of Zender Eichbaum, we may return. . . ." "How did Benya Krik, gangster and king of gangsters, become Eichbaum's son-in law? How did he become son-in-law of a man who owned sixty milk cows minus one?" "Here is what the foaming surge of the Odessa sea bears to the shore, here is what *{ vot chto}*. . . ." One story, "Kak eto delalos v Odesse" (How it was done in Odessa), a more obvious enactment of oral speech, is told by a character, Arye-Leib, a bard of the underworld. In the manner of oral narration, the stories are loosely strung together. There are frequent digressions, stories within stories, the entire cycle ends with a promise of other tales to be told in an unfolding *comédie humaine* of the Moldavanka: "if I am able, I will tell them all one after the other, for they are very entertaining tales" (*I*, 160–62, 188).[1]

"How did Benya Krik, gangster and king of gangsters, become Eichbaum's son-in-law?" introduces a story within the opening story, "Korol" (The king), and the other three follow this folklorish formula, relating how a state of affairs came to be. In "How It Was Done in Odessa" Arye-Leib recounts with admiration the story of Benya Krik's rise to the top of the heap, or how Benya became "King." A council of gangsters puts Benya to the test of doing a job on one Ruvim Tartakovsky. Now, the denizens of Babel's Moldavanka are not run-of-the-mill mortals, they are "characters," cartoons from the pen of a Russian-Jewish Damon Runyon. The victim Tartakovsky is as hyperbolically drawn as Benya, his victimizer. Known as the "Jew-and-a-Half" for his physical size, daring, and wealth, Tartakovsky has become a favorite challenge for the enterprising mobsters of Odessa, which earns him the less enviable so-

briquet of "Nine Holdups." Benya's makes ten! Benya is a crook
with a heart of gold, a Jewish Robin Hood, who threatens more
violence than he actually delivers. When in the course of the holdup
the trigger-happy gunman Savka Butsis shoots and kills the frightened clerk Muginstein, Benya's sense of fair play is outraged. To
pay Paul he robs Peter, extorting enough cash from Tartakovsky to
provide for Muginstein's bereaved mother and for a funeral that
would do honor to a head of state. After delivering an eloquent
though semiliterate funeral oration, he announces that the clerk's
killer has also been dispatched to his final resting place. The crowd—
all Jewish Odessa seems to have shown up—promptly proceeds to
a second funeral, the likes of which "Savka had never dreamed."

"Otets" (The father) tells of Froim Grach, an aging gangster,
who marries off his sex-starved amazon of a daughter. Badgered by
the young woman to find her a husband capable of quenching her
desires, Froim calls upon the Capons, whose son has shown interest
in that task. The Capons are storekeepers, who, true to their name,
care much less for romantic passion than for middle-class respectability, and Froim is more than Mme Capon can stomach. Benya
comes to the rescue. He will marry the amorous Basya himself and,
in addition, will compel the Capons to fork over two thousand
rubles as compensation for Basya's humiliating rejection. "With
God's help," he tells his father-in-law-to-be, "we will show all
grocers where to get off."

Benya vanishes from "Lyubka Kazak" (Lyubka the Cossack), another "how" story: how the salesman Tsudechkis, small in stature
but great in courage, becomes the manager of Lyubka's combination
inn, grain store, smuggler's den, and whorehouse. Lyubka is Jewish;
"Cossack" is a nickname bestowed on her for her unusual physical
proportions. She is another amazon (Babel was taken by the type)
with mountainous breasts. Despite her ample equipment, she ne-
glects to nurse her child, who has anyhow grown too big even for
her lavish breasts. Tsudechkis fearlessly denounces her dereliction
of maternal duty with prophetic Jewish righteousness, then weans
her overgrown baby by a clever trick. His ingenious daring wins
him a perhaps unenviable position as Lyubka's manager.

The "how" story inserted into "The King" is a flashback. The
social barriers that restrain the rest of us do not hold for Benya.
Zender Eichbaum is a wealthy man, the proud possessor of sixty
milk cows minus one, while Benya is poor. Crime brings them

together. While slaughtering Eichbaum's cows to extort protection payoffs—the most violent act we see him perform—Benya catches sight of Eichbaum's lovely daughter clad in a scanty nightgown, "and the victory of the King became his defeat" (the discrepancy of two wives in two stories is never accounted for). The major plot of "The King" turns on an incident from Benya's comic career. Officiating at the wedding ceremony of his forty-year-old sex-starved sister (yet another!) and a timid young man he has bribed to marry her, Benya learns that an ambitious new police captain is planning to raid the proceedings. Benya is "King," and the captain holds that "where there's an emperor [i.e., the czar], there's no room for a king." Benya greets the news with regal nonchalance. After the digression on Eichbaum's cows and daughter, the scene shifts back to Dvoyra's wedding, as a gleeful messenger bursts in to report that the police station is in flames and the raid is off. Benya is not in the least surprised. The story ends with the ravenous Dvoyra dragging her terrified husband off to the marriage bed "like a cat, who, holding a mouse in its jaws, tests it gingerly with its teeth."

Babel's prose is as playful as his plots. He employs a highly ornamental style derived from symbolism—unusual metaphors, colorful imagery, synesthesia, personification, rhythmic phrasing, parallels, and repetitions—in a context of Hogarthian naturalism. His mixed manner lowers symbolist solemnity to whimsy. The charm is in the excess.

The wedding ceremony was over, the Rabbi lowered himself into an armchair. Then, going outside, he viewed the tables arrayed the length of the courtyard. The row was so long that it poked its tail through the gates into Hospital Street. Velvet-spread, the tables wound their way down the yard like so many snakes with varicolored patches on their bellies, and they sang full-throatedly, those patches of orange and red velvet.
     . . . A thick flame beat through the sooty doors, a flame drunken and puffy-lipped. The faces of old crones broiled in its smoky rays—old women's quivering chins and beslobbered bosoms. Sweat, as pink as blood, as pink as the slaver of a mad dog, streamed over these mounds of exorbitant and sweetly pungent human flesh. . . . over all the cooks and dishwashers reigned the eighty-year-old Reyzl, tiny and humpbacked, as traditional as a scroll of the Torah. (*I*, 159)

As in Gogol's prose, the extensive detail is so quirky—tables winding their way like serpents, singing patches on their bellies—as itself to become an object of interest. Language is more than a transparent medium through which we view things; it shapes an intricate stained-glass window whose colorful patterns command attention in their own right. The world is present but comically deformed.

Babel's dialogue is as artificial as his narration. Speech takes the form of ritualized gestures and folksy aphorisms: "Take me on. I want to moor my boat to your shore. The shore I moor my boat to will be a winner"; "Who are you, where do you come from and what do you use for breath?"; "Try me out, . . . and let's stop smearing gruel over a clean table"; "Let's stop smearing gruel, . . . I'll give you a try" (I, 166).

The narrator plays with his characters so as to explode the illusion of their reality, making us aware that they are creatures of his art, figures in an aesthetic design:

[Froim] heard him out patiently but then interrupted, because he was a simple man without guile.
"I am a simple man without guile," said Froim. (I, 177)

Benya, the star of the cycle, is a concoction of comic fancy. With his almost edible outfit of chocolate jacket, cream pants, and raspberry boots, with his red automobile equipped with a horn that toots "Laugh, clown" from *Pagliacci,* he is a genuine cartoon. A figure of grand gestures and grandiloquent speech, he would feel at home in comic opera—Babel refers to one of his stunts as "an opera in three acts" (I, 168)—or in its American derivative, the Broadway musical.

The Cossacks of *Red Cavalry* can also be extravagantly operatic, and the narrator views their roosterlike strutting with the same mixture of admiration and bemused irony he displays toward Benya. But the violence of the Cossacks is serious and awful. Reality intrudes into *Red Cavalry* in a way it does not in *Odessa Tales,* and as a result Babel was compelled in the later cycle to open his decorative design to genuine moral issues. In *Odessa Tales* violence is mostly verbal bluster. If people are killed it is a clumsy accident (Muginstein) or offstage (Savka Butsis). As Benya's musical automobile erupts into "Laugh, clown," we half expect funny flags to burst out of his revolver as in the circus. *Red Cavalry* is an epic of war and revolution; *Odessa Tales* is a mock epic of Jewish ghetto life.

The mock epic or mock heroic treats the small in large terms. It employs more ammunition than its target requires, with artillery wheeled on stage to kill a fly. The discrepancy between threat and actuality makes Benya a comic figure, as does the gap between his rhetorical grandiloquence, much of it couched in street jargon, and the occasions when he exercises it. In a nutshell, Benya talks funny. Babel's comic gift lies in words, not incidents. Benya's funeral oration for the hapless Muginstein is a highlight of the cycle:

Ladies and gentlemen and dames. . . . What did our dear Joseph get out of life? A hill of beans. How did he spend his time? Counting other people's cash. What did he perish for? He perished for the whole of the working class. There are people already condemned to death, and there are people who have not yet begun to live. . . . There are people who don't know how to drink vodka, and there are people who don't know how to drink vodka but drink it anyhow. And the thing is the first lot get satisfaction from joy and from sorrow, and the second lot suffer for all those who drink vodka and don't know how. And so, ladies and gentlemen and dames. . . . *(I, 172)*

Mock epic is a species of parody. It juxtaposes the literary modes of epic grandeur and homely realism. Parody may be derisive, but it is not necessarily so. In its etymology it simply denotes two songs placed side by side (Greek *para ōide*). Two juxtaposed styles or viewpoints may interact in complex ways, as in *Don Quixote,* where the Don's romantic illusions founder against real windmills and yet endow his character with imaginative richness. Moldavanka is a confined ghetto populated by the ignorant poor clutching, like the rest of us, at whatever happiness they can wrest from life. Benya's ambitions go no further than his cholocate jacket, raspberry boots, and the red car with the operatic horn. By investing the language of this intellectually limited man with overblown grandiosity and by treating his milieu with analogous epic amplitude, Babel inevitably throws an ironic light on his subject. Benya's eloquence is misplaced. Muginstein did not die "for the whole of the working class"; he was the victim of Benya's own holdup! But the double vision of parody results in a double response. Benya is funny because he speaks and lives out of proportion with his circumstances, but his grand gestures also lend him charm. His appeal is that of a man who refuses to be what he ought to be—it is the appeal of freedom.

Likewise the wedding of the predatory forty-year-old virgin Dvoyra, perched upon a mountain of cushions like some pagan queen, her timorous groom quaking at her side, the cortege of gaudily dressed gangsters bringing gifts, though comic, is also celebrative. A secondary meaning of "to mock," besides "to ridicule," is "to mimic" or "to play at," and the rowdy mobsters of Moldavanka play at being knights of romance. They perform with more gusto than grace, but vitality has its own attractions. The scene is reminiscent of the wedding feast that opens Gogol's "The Terrible Vengeance," except that where Gogol is ultimately punitive, arranging it so that diabolical intervention cuts short the gay abandon of his revelers, Babel lets his people have their fun.

The rejoicings reached their pitch when, according to the custom of olden times, the guests began bestowing their wedding gifts. One shammes from the synagogue after another leaped on a table and, to the clamorous roar of the fanfare, sang out how many rubles, how many silver spoons.

And now the friends of the King showed the worth of blue blood, of the chivalry, not yet extinct, of the Moldavanka. On silver trays, with nonchalant movements of the hand, they cast golden coins, rings, threaded coral.

Aristocrats of the Moldavanka, they were tightly encased in raspberry waistcoats. Russet jackets clasped their shoulders, and on their meaty feet the leather, azure as the sky, cracked. Rising to their full height and thrusting out their bellies, the bandits slapped their palms in time to the music, cried out "Kiss, kiss!" and showered the bride with blossoms. And she, Dvoyra of forty summers, sister to the King, disfigured by illness, with swollen crop and eyes bulging from their orbits, sat on a mountain of cushions side by side with the feeble young man, purchased by Eichbaum's cash and mute with misery. *(I, 162–63)*

Comic characters usually have something serious to say even in spite of themselves. Benya rejects Jewish suffering. He would take life as it is, getting his "satisfaction from joy and from sorrow." If God has decreed misery, then God is in error: "But wasn't it a mistake on the part of God to settle the Jews in Russia, for them to be tormented worse than in Hell? How would it hurt if the Jews lived in Switzerland, where they would be surrounded by first-class lakes, mountain air, and Frenchies as thick as flies. All make mistakes, God not excepted" *(I, 170–71)*. Benya is a rebel, but a Jewish rebel, identifying entirely with the Jewish world of Moldavanka. If asked whether he wished to be something other than Jewish he would find the question incomprehensible. To be sure, he has turned his back on Jewish orthodoxy, which sought to dignify suffering as the price of God's design for his chosen people, but even in his rebellion he reflects another Jewish tradition, the plebeian iconoclasm and earthy realism of Jewish folk humor and Yiddish writing that grows out of it. Complaints against God are common to both and, unlike what we find in the Book of Job, God does not always have the last word.[2] Jewish humor has flowed like an underground stream, offering refreshment from ethical seriousness and nourishment to ordinary men and women in their embattled lives. "Jewish humor typically draws the charge of cosmic significance from suffering by grounding it in a world of homely practical realities," as Robert Alter puts it.[3]

Practical realities are manageable. Benya knows the world is rotten, but he feels he can do something about it, if only in his own narrow sphere. Though his cocky defiance sets him apart from that typical figure of Jewish humor the schlemiel, the two are cousins. The schlemiel shows the world a face of bumbling innocence, but through guile or sheer patience born of acceptance of life manages to turn his defeats into victories. Benya is like him, and like countless comic figures in other national literatures. Often silly, he finds a way to come out on top. He asserts the power of life against fantasies of perfection, comedy's first enemy.

Benya's foil is the narrator. A stand-in for the author, he is an intellectual and a writer. "Benya Krik had his way," he tells us, "for he was passionate, and passion rules the universe." The narrator appreciates the passionate universe but is temperamentally unable to enter it. The ironies turn against the literary process itself, which is viewed as hopeless voyeurism. Benya acts and hence lives, whereas the writer substitutes words for action and lives only vicariously. Arye-Leib, in recounting how Benya became King, tells him to "forget for a while that you have spectacles on your nose and autumn in your heart. Stop carrying on at your desk and stammering among people. Imagine for a moment that you're carrying on in public and stammering on paper. . . . how would you have acted in Benya's place? You don't know how you would have acted. But he knew. That's why he's the King, while you and I are sitting on the wall of the Second Jewish Cemetery and keeping the sun off with our palms." He concludes: "Now you know all. . . . you know all.

But what's the use, if you still have spectacles on your nose and autumn in your heart?" (*I*, 162, 165–66, 169, 173). Like the author of Genesis, Babel chooses the Tree of Life over the Tree of Knowledge. In dissociating "life" from ethical commands he is, however, more pagan than Jewish. For the frothy fancies of *Odessa Tales* such a position might be adequate. But he could not hold to it when confronted with the tragic crisis of war and revolution.

Chapter Five
Miscellaneous Stories (1923–25)

Revolutions are by nature iconoclastic. Sons take revenge on their fathers, the younger generation throws overboard the baggage of the old, the spirit of rebellion says that anything goes. The early years of the Revolution, before the bureaucrats had their way, unloosed great stores of creative energy in the Soviet Union. The crumbling of traditional restraints led to to a more uninhibited treatment of sex (continuing the bold explorations of the prewar modernists) than had been the norm for Russian culture. Along with Eros dark forces of destruction surfaced. Babel shared the epoch's fascination with sex and violence, but his disciplined intellectual control usually (though not always) kept him from its excesses. He also took himself less seriously than many of his critics have. Sex could be a matter of urgency, but also a source of fun.

"Iisusov grekh" (The sin of Jesus, 1924) is a fable stylized in the manner of folk literature. One of the many ways writers of the twenties rebelled against symbolism was to replace allegory with folksy yarns. Aleksey Remizov, another master of *skaz*, provided a model for this kind of writing; his star pupil Zamyatin wrote a number of such fables. Where symbolist allegory is portentous, "The Sin of Jesus" is ironic. The fable's contenders are the body and the soul, and, true to the disposition of the times, the body gets the better of the argument. The prose is patterned upon the diction and rhythmic phrasing of folk tales: "Arina lived in a hotel off the main staircase, while Seryoga, the janitor's helper, lived over the back stairs. Between them there was shame. On Palm Sunday Arina gave Seryoga a present of twins. Water flows, stars shine, a man lusts." As the waters flow, Arina accumulates pregnancies: "To work in a hotel is to live with your skirt turned up. Whoever stops in—he's your lord and master, may he be a Jew, may he be anybody at all."

Weary of abusive men, Arina appeals to Jesus; her lament turns into a folklorish refrain: "To live in a hotel . . . ," etc. The encounter between the Son of God and the woman who cannot say no is done in homely style, lowering spiritual drama to playful comedy. The woman gets the best lines. When Jesus prescribes four years of abstinence, Arina is flabbergasted: "Four years? To hear you talk, people ought to give up their animal natures {razzhivo-titsya}. For you that's an old habit. But where will offspring come from? No, make some sense and relieve my misery." The Son of God remembers an angel named Alfred who has been moping around heaven, complaining that he has been elevated from his earthly condition too soon. In His infinite mercy He bestows Alfred on long-suffering Arina: "He is your prayer, he is your protection, he is your lover." Even better, Alfred can do no damage, "for there's much sport in him but no seriousness." Folk tales, however, sadly include a prohibition: Arina must remove Alfred's wings each night because, made of children's sighs, they are very delicate.

Arina suffers all the frailties of the flesh. She is a creature of this world, of messy imperfect life: "Not enough for her to sleep with an angel, not enough that nobody beside her spat at the wall, snored and snorted—that wasn't enough for this hot, ravenous woman." In her lust she mounts Alfred, crushing him. When Jesus loses patience and condemns Arina to the prison of her body, she rebels, refusing responsibility for her fallen condition: "Was it I who made this heavy body of mine? Was it I who brewed vodka on earth? Was it I who created a woman's body, stupid and lonely?" Arina goes back to lifting her skirts for one and all, while Babel announces: "And that's the end of my tale."

It is regrettably not the end. Arina returns to Jesus, pregnant again, to complain of her suffering. Jesus weeps: "Forgive me, Arina, forgive your sinful God for all He has done to you." Arina is unrelenting: "There is no forgiveness for you, Jesus Christ, and never will be" (I, 204–8). That blasphemy is in the spirit of the times, as is the humanistic moral. The message is also unearned and hence sentimental, for Arina enjoys her "sufferings" too much to stand as a female Job. The story would have been better left at Babel's earlier announcement of a conclusion. Up to there it is a lovely piece of work, written in brilliant prose that is at once poetical and delightfully ironic.

"Skazka pro babu" (Tale of a woman, 1923) has some resemblances to "The Sin of Jesus." It is another *skaz* improvised in the manner of the folk tale, this time in a farcical vein: "Once upon a time there lived a woman named Ksenya. Big bosom, round shoulders, blue eyes." While Arina "suffers" from too much sexual activity, Ksenya, a servant for a rich family, suffers from too little. Her husband has been killed in the war, she complains of headaches, a doctor recommends she take a man: "I wouldn't dare," she protests, "I'm too delicate." Nevertheless, a local sorceress (*znakharka*), Grandma Morozikha, comes up with a candidate who, unfortunately, turns out to be even more delicate than Ksenya. Valentin is a bit of a poet—he makes up songs, and a bit of a madman—when he drinks he is possessed by odd visions. A bastard son of a member of the gentry, he takes pride in his noble ancestry. What he cannot (or will not) do is perform in bed. Like the angel Alfred, he has sport in him but no seriousness. Ksenya's employer sees the drunken Valentin being carried from the house and dismisses her for participation in an orgy which never occurred, and Grandma Morozikha formulates the moral of the tale: "It was a mistake. What we needed was someone simpler. We should have gotten Mityukha." In Babel's fiction the sensitive poets never measure up. They may sing good songs but they do not get the girl.[1]

"Bagrat-Ogly i glaza ego byka" (Bagrat-Ogly and the eyes of his bull, 1923) is an unusual work for Babel. Early Soviet writing often merged symbolist mannerisms into a naturalistic context, but "Bagrat-Ogly" is pure fable at a high level of abstraction, which places it closer to symbolism than anything else Babel wrote. An exotic "Eastern" tale set in Anatolia, it tells of one Bagrat-Ogly whose prize bull is gelded by an envious neighbor. Though Babel often builds a story so as to lead up to the narrator's concluding ruminations, the reality he describes retains its integrity, but here it is mere fuel for his meditations. Bagrat-Ogly and his fellow Muslim tribesmen—from a culture Babel did not know or much care about—are evoked solely so that he may indulge in some colorful writing and reflect on man's malice.[2]

Babel wrote several stories about his Civil War experience that he omitted from *Red Cavalry*. In the case of "U batki nashego Makhno" (With Old Man Makhno, 1924), one can see why. The material is brutal even by the standards of that work, a crude vehicle for heavy-handed irony. A freakish young man complains to a bovine

Jewish girl of his hard lot on Makhno's staff: it seems that on the previous night six of Makhno's men had raped the poor woman, neglecting to give our Lothario his turn. The young man decides "each has a heart of stone." What the girl thinks of his callous recitation we do not discover. Instead of attempting to catch her suffering, Babel indulges in an elaborate image: "The Jewish girl raised her blood-suffused face from the tub, glanced at the boy, and went out of the kitchen with the awkward gait of a cavalryman when he puts his numbed legs on the ground after a long ride." Babel sometimes (though not too often) lets his style run away with his story. The tale concludes with the mean-spirited clown, oblivious of the effect of his whining monologue, blithely walking around the room on his hands. If there are those who believe that Babel really saw the Cossacks as noble savages, "With Old Man Makhno" should disabuse them of that conviction.[3]

The cart driver Grishchuk appears in several stories from *Red Cavalry,* and in one of them ("The death of Dolgushov") he performs an act of kindness. Seeing Lyutov in despair at his inability to finish off the mortally wounded Dolgushov, which earns him the hatred of his Cossack friend Afonka Bida, Grishchuk offers Lyutov an apple as a token of comradeship. Perhaps Babel omitted the story devoted to this gentle man ("Grishchuk" [1923]) because he thought it too sketchy. If so, he was wrong. In the notebook he kept while serving with the First Cavalry Army, Babel asked, "What is Grishchuk? Eternal silence, limitless apathy." The story depicts him that way, and then recounts his experiences as a prisoner of war in forced labor to a German farmer. The German is as silent as he, and mad to boot. He starves and beats his prisoner. The little communicating they do is by sign language. When the war ends and Grishchuk prepares to go home, the demented master and his long-suffering servant join in a silent embrace of farewell. Two strange men, enemies, unequal in station, unable to speak to each other, have yet felt each other's humanity. "Grishchuk" does more honor to the mystery of human personality than many longer works by lesser writers.[4]

"Ikh bylo devyat" (There were nine, 1923) is an earlier version of "Eskadronny Trunov" (Squadron Commander Trunov) of *Red Cavalry.* Each describes the murder of Polish prisoners of war by a member of Budyonny's Cavalry—Corporal Golov in the former, Trunov in the latter. Babel may have discarded his first effort out of fear of the censors for it is openly sympathetic to the victims, ending with a pledge to "do something in memory of them." Or he may simply have been dissatisfied with it, since his almost total concentration on the anguish of the narrator gives it a narrow scope. It is the kind of story that can be easily pigeonholed: sensitive Jewish intellectual encounters the horrors of war. A comparison to "Squadron Commander Trunov" is instructive. Here Babel enlarges his tale in a way characteristic of *Red Cavalry*, and observes Trunov more carefully than his predecessor. Still a brutal, bloody fellow, he is also capable of grandly heroic gestures, even inexplicably choosing his own death. Though the lyrical strain by no means disappears from *Red Cavalry*, the field of action has become panoramic, "epical," less subjective. The narrator again expresses his outrage, but his presence is only one brush stroke on a canvas teeming with life: solemn Cossack horsemen, quarreling Orthodox and Hasidic Jews, Polish prisoners, mercenaries who fly American bombers. The difference between "There Were Nine" and "Squadron Commander Trunov" is that between a lesson in morality and a moment in human history.[5]

In the Soviet Union Babel is regarded as a "Soviet writer," and correctly so. Not a mere geographic designation, the term indicates that a writer has passed a loyalty test. Of course everything depends on who does the grading. The neutral observer can only say that Babel saw himself as part of his society, and others saw him that way too. Even in Stalin's time, though he was severely criticized, his membership in the culture was unquestioned. True, he was eventually arrested and probably shot, but in the late thirties state terror had grown to such epidemic proportions that no one was safe. Though he shared the aspirations of his revolutionary society, only a few of his works display the explicit propagandistic intent of stories like "Konets sv. Ipatiya" (The end of St. Hypatius, 1924) and "Ty promorgal, kapitan" (You were too trusting, captain, 1924) *(I, 227–31)*.

Close in style and theme to the *Red Cavalry* stories, "The End of St. Hypatius" ends on an upbeat note quite uncharacteristic of that book. The narrator visits the monastery of St. Hypatius, where in 1613 the people of Moscow beseeched the first Romanov, Mikhail, to accept the throne of Muscovy. Like other churches in Babel's fiction, St. Hypatius is in decay but beautiful. It is also a quintessentially Russian place—brilliantly colored, ominous in the mem-

ories it conveys of brutal Russian history, "of a holiness that knew
no mercy," yet as unpretentious as the pancakes of Russian fields
with their decorated peasant huts. "Crowned with a wreath of snow,
painted with crimson and azure, it rose against the smoky northern
sky like a peasant woman's many-colored kerchief embroidered with
Russian flowers," Babel writes. The narrator's eye roams over a scene
that might have been painted by a Russian Breughel: the ice-clad
Volga, cart horses pulling sledges, crowds of peasant women. Russia,
it seems, has not changed: " 'Devils,' I cried. . . . 'Are you coming
to Marfa the Nun, to entreat for her son Mikhail Romanov as czar?' "
But the narrator is mistaken. The peasant women are actually members of the Union of Textile Workers on their way to expropriate
the ancient monastery. In *Red Cavalry* such contrasts between the
old and the new are utilized to explore the tragic and sometimes
comic incongruities of an era of revolutionary change. In "St. Hypatius" the narrative resolves itself in a purple patch of panegyric:
"a young man who refused to lose heart was stubbornly trying to
clamber up the frozen ladder . . . in order to hang up a meager
little lamp and a signboard on which were inscribed the multitu-
dinous letters USSR and RSFSR, and the emblem of the Textile
Union, and the sickle and hammer, and a portrait of a woman
standing at a loom from which rays shot in all directions." It is a
mark of Babel's discipline as a writer that nothing like "St. Hypatius" found its way into *Red Cavalry,* which he was composing
simultaneously. For all its lovely descriptions, it belongs in *Pravda,*
where indeed it was first published.

Babel seems to have admired Lenin; or at least, he liked his prose,
"the secret curve of Lenin's straight line" *(I, 56).* "You Were Too
Trusting, Captain" is a tribute to him. On the day of Lenin's funeral,
in Odessa, an international crew of a Malay, three Chinese, and two
Negroes, assisted by a white boatswain, sneak off an English freighter
to attend a ceremony in his honor. In a display of proletarian sol-
idarity they are greeted by a band of Russian stevedores. Meanwhile,
the too trusting captain, unaware that his men have gone ashore
without permission, sits in his cabin, smoking cigars and sipping
brandy, alone. Was Babel serious about this sort of pap? All one
can say is that, while in the thirties they might keep a man out of
prison or save his life, in the early twenties writers could and did
avoid such public demonstrations of allegiance.

"Zakat" (Sunset, written in 1924–25) continues the Odessa cycle, deriving from a passing comment in "The Father": "Mendel Krik sat at one of the tables drinking wine from a green tumbler and relating how he had been crippled by his own sons—the elder Benya and the younger Lyovka." In "Sunset" Benya and Lyovka plot to kill their tyrannical father, Mendel the drayman. Since the mode is still comic, they are not permitted to carry out such a horrendous act, but merely succeed in getting their sister, the love-starved virgin Dvoyra, to whack him over the head with a colander. Mendel's pride as well as his skull are wounded. He recognizes that his sun has set and turns over the business, which is in disarray, to the boys. Benya puts things in order and arranges a celebration to pay homage to his father, or at least the principle of paternity. Whatever his faults, Mendel has suffered like any man, and especially a Jew. "Sunset" is weaker than the other *Odessa* tales, and Babel did not publish it. It has its moments of fun and its share of colorful writing, though that is at times forced, even in bad taste: "Stars—green stars on a dark-blue background—were scattered in front of the window like soldiers relieving themselves."[6] Mendel and his sons are too nasty to be endearing. Perhaps Babel was getting weary of the old formulas, or he may have intended his piece only as a preliminary sketch for a play he wrote with the same title. The play, as we shall see, is much more interesting, for here Babel realizes that Mendel's situation is more pathetic than funny.

Babel found prostitutes intriguing. He wrote about them in the early "Ilya Isaakovich and Margarita Prokofevna," and again in "Khodya" (1923) and "V shcholochku" (Through the fanlight, 1924). Neither displays the artistry Babel had achieved by the mid-twenties, which suggests they may have been products of an earlier period pulled out of the desk drawer for publication. "Khodya" bears the subtitle, "From the book *Petersburg 1918.*" It is sordid stuff. In famine struck St. Petersburg a Chinaman buys a prostitute's favors for a loaf of bread, then afterward he presses the girl's philosophizing godfather upon her. The story's tone recalls the nightmarish prose of Andrey Bely (the godfather even speaks of the Reds as Mongols, as did Bely of the revolutionaries of his day, confirming the suspicion that the story dates from a time when Babel had not yet found his own style): "A dead man's fingers were picking at the frozen entrails of St. Petersburg. . . . Black vials of ink burst in the sky."[7]

"Through the Fanlight" is also an urban story. The city is un-
named, but since the narrator's activity is the kind of thing one
usually gets over after adolescence, we may guess it is Odessa. Our
hero spies on the prostitute Marusya through a fanlight. The woman
seems genuinely in love with one of her clients, a nondescript, lanky
fellow, who carefully squeezes a pimple from under his moustache
before hopping into bed. Such are the ways of love.[8]

Chapter Six
Red Cavalry

For all their charm, *Odessa Tales* still smack of the provincialism of the genre sketch. *Red Cavalry* is a work of sophisticated maturity. The most important fiction to come out of the Russian Revolution— its only real competitor is a poem, Blok's *The Twelve*—it can advance a claim to stand as the national epic of that momentous event. *Red Cavalry* is to the Russian Revolution what Tolstoy's *War and Peace* is to the Napoleonic invasion, an attempt of the literary imagination to grasp a climactic historical experience in the life of a people. Of course Tolstoy's novel is broader in scope and deeper in its penetration of human experience. Also, the two authors come out of markedly different traditions: Tolstoy is the supreme master of the realistic novel, while Babel proceeds from the imperatives of modernism. Tolstoy offers a microcosm of the world that is comprehensive, exhaustive, and psychologically persuasive. Babel is fragmentary, elliptical, elusive, very much a modernist in his tendency to decompose a text into pastiche. Less confident than his nineteenth-century predecessors about the susceptibility of the world to systematic description, he regards reality more as a mystery to be intuited than a puzzle to be solved. As a result his fiction is metaphoric rather than explicative, suggestive instead of analytical. It narrows character to a figure in a pattern that is at once highly decorative and rich in implication. Even as it presents the world piecemeal, *Red Cavalry* yet betrays a Tolstoyan aspiration to show it in its entirety, to create an epic of a decisive historical moment.

Though *Red Cavalry* may leave an initial impression of a medley of sketches, Babel conceived it as a whole. He worried about the ordering of the individual stories, which he called "excerpts" and "chapters" of a book.[1] A collection on a single topic will inevitably have a kind of unity—that of the cycle or anthology—but *Red Cavalry* is more tightly knit than that. Most of the stories are told by a stand-in for the author, Lyutov (Babel's alias while serving with the First Cavalry Army). Since the actors are mostly unlettered soldiers, Lyutov's mediating consciousness serves to color and complicate bare events with the reflections of a poet's sensibility. As in a travel book, our attention is focused on both scene and narrator. In the setting of the Polish campaign of 1920, the two cultures the Cossack army comes in contact with—Catholic Poland and the Jewish Pale of Settlement—are, like Odessa's Moldavanka, distanced from the reader, made strange.[2] Lyutov guides us through the unfamiliar terrain of war and the exotic landscapes in which it is conducted. His response is a tale in itself. *Red Cavalry* is thirty-five stories, but it is also a single story, a kind of novel relating one man's passage through war and revolution.

The *Skaz* Tales

Aside from Lyutov, the narrators are soldiers, mostly Cossacks. They speak or write (some of their tales are in the form of letters) in substandard Russian mixed with local dialectisms. In the tradition of *skaz* from Gogol and Leskov through the 1920s, when the manner became highly popular (in the work of Zamyatin, Zoshchenko, Ilf and Petrov), a peculiar idiom is not merely replicated but manipulated for comic and ironic effects. The ironies stem from a deformation of language.

The Cossacks are men of large gesture and small vision. The accidents of history have cast them as actors in an epoch-making drama. Only dimly aware of its awesomeness, their minds cluttered with revolutionary slogans and the bric-a-brac of Communist ideology, they yet insist upon their more tangible claims of personal honor, revenge, and plunder. Their speech resolves into a kind of oxymoron, a comical combination of disparate items: "Let us die for a sour pickle and the world revolution" (*I*, 88).

In "Pismo" (A letter) a callow youth writes to his mother of his father's murder by the boy's brother. The father is in turn the murderer of another brother (the father is a White; the sons, Reds). The young man narrates these brutal events in a chillingly matter-of-fact manner, placing a value on the life of his horse that he denies his father. His language is a concatenation of revolutionary bombast, homely colloquialisms, and Gogolian non sequiturs: "They took me into the expeditionary Political Section where we hand out reading material and newspapers to the positions—the *Moscow Izvestiya* of the Central Executive Committee, *Moscow Pravda*, and our homebred merciless paper, *The Red Cavalry Man*, which every fighting man on the front lines hungers to read and after that with heroic spirit he cuts down the rotten Poles, and I'm living at Nikon Vasilevich's in grand style."

"Zhizneopisanie Pavlichenki, Matveya Rodionycha" (The life and adventures of Matvey Pavlichenko) tells of Matvey's vengeance on his pre-Revolutionary master, who had taken advantage of his wife and then struck him when he dared complain. The story is a fable on the making of a revolutionary warrior, detailing Matvey's progress from submissiveness to violent aggression or, to use the tale's metaphors, from herdsman to "wolf" and "jackal." Though the action is terribly brutal, the tone is closer to "black comedy" than melodrama. The language, which plays upon oratorical hyperbole grounded in colloquialisms and folklorish turns, is a richer and more imaginative elaboration of the mock-epic style of *Odessa Tales*:

Countrymen, comrades, my own dear brothers! In the name of all mankind learn the life story of the Red General Matvey Pavlichenko. He used to be a herdsman, that general did, a herdsman on the Lidino estate, for Nikitinsky the master, and he looked after the master's pigs till life brought stripes to his shoulder straps; and then with those stripes of his Matyushka began to look after horned cattle. And who knows, if this Matvey of ours had been born in Australia, then chances are, my friends, he might have been elevated to elephants, our Matyushka would have come to grazing elephants; only the trouble is where would you find elephants in our district of Stavropol.

In a third example of *skaz,* "Izmena" (Treason), a Cossack accused of disorderly conduct protests his and his comrades' innocence in a letter to a police investigator. The comedy, much like Zoshchenko's, turns on the clash of two cultures: the bureaucratized routines of institutions and the personalistic ethos of people not yet assimilated into modern ways. The Cossacks when sent to a hospital misconstrue conventional regulations as treason to revolutionary militancy, refuse to surrender their arms, and raise havoc. As in much of *skaz* literature, the laugh is, so to speak, behind the back of the narrator. Since we readers move within the normative sphere of rules and regulations, we view the Cossack's complaint from the perspective of his straight victims. From the vantage point of ordinary life and language the narrator appears as comically out of place as a Gargantua among pygmies: "we disarmed the militia in the form of one fellow on horseback, and destroyed with tears in our eyes three mediocre windows in the above-described storeroom. . . . In his short Red life Comrade Kustov was real upset about the treason that is now winking at us from the window, now making game of the common proletariat, but the proletariat, comrades, knows it is common, it hurts us, it does, and our souls burn and burst with flames the prison of our body. Treason, I tell you, Comrade Investigator Burdenko, treason laughs at us from the window, treason is going about the house barefoot, treason has taken off its boots so the floorboards in the burgled house won't creak."

Though distanced from us by comedy, the Cossacks are not simply objects of ridicule, nor are the author's ironies morally disapproving. Like Benya Krik, their Jewish literary cousin, they are outsized men, sometimes comically odd, sometimes frightening in their violence, but passionate and heroic. Uninhibited by the restraints of conventional society, they yet hold to codes of honor and the dictates of principle. The family of "A Letter" is shockingly brutish, but its members act from a sense of justice (*pravda*).[3] Set against each other by politics and personal animosity, both father and sons acquire dignity from the knowledge that were the tables turned, were victim to become victimizer, they would behave no differently. They fully accept the terms of their world. Matvey Pavlichenko's vengeance is horrifying. Underlying his abandon to violence, however, there is again a principle—that a man ought to enter into a personal relationship even with his enemy, no matter at what cost to himself. Not for Matvey are the abstract devices of modern warfare: "Then I stomped on my master Nikitinsky. I trampled him for an hour or maybe more. And in that time I got to know life through and through. With shooting . . . you only can get rid of a man. Shooting's letting him off, and too damn easy for yourself. With shooting you'll never get at the soul, to where it is in a man and how it shows itself. But I don't spare myself. . . . I want to get to know what life really is, what life's like down our way."

Epos

The stories told by the sophisticated Lyutov-Babel touch a wider range of experience and gamut of styles than the *skaz* tales: factual reportage, naturalistic description, lyrical meditation, poetic evocation, wry irony, heroic hyperbole. Schematically these divide into two—the style of war and the style of culture, corresponding to what Renato Poggioli has called the "epic-heroic" and the "pathetic."[4] War rips a breach in the settled ways of culture, a revolutionary war even more so, since it assaults its very foundations. The dictionary definition of revolution is "momentous change," and change is the stuff of history. Change does violence to the existing order of things. It has its agents and its patients, those who introduce the new and those who suffer it.

The epic mode is one of action. Its rhythms resemble a drum beat—loud, insistent, constant. Armies are on the move, altering the face of history. From the march of revolution and war, running through the book like a line, if interrupted then inevitably resumed, curves veer away to chart scenes from the ordinary life of culture. Here the victims of history are to be found.

In "Perekhod cherez Zbruch" (Crossing into Poland) the Cossacks burst onto the scene (and into the book) in a riot of color, sound, and movement.

Fields of crimson poppy flower around us, a noon-time breeze plays in the yellowing rye, virginal buckwheat looms on the horizon like the wall of a distant monastery. The silent Volyn bends, the Volyn moves away from us into the pearly haze of birch groves, it crawls into the flowering hills and with loosening arms entangles itself in thickets of hops. An orange sun rolls along the sky like a lopped-off head, a tender light flares in the gorges of clouds, the standards of the sunset fly over our heads. The smell of yesterday's blood and of slaughtered horses drips into the evening chill. The blackened Zbruch roars and twists the foamy knots of its rapids. The bridges are down, and we ford the river. A majestic moon rests on the waves. The horses enter the water to their cruppers, the resounding torrents run through hundreds of horses' legs. Someone sinks and loudly curses the Mother of God. The river is strewn with black squares of wagons, it is full of clamour, whistles, and songs, thundering above the serpentine trails of the moon and the luminous hollows.

Though the imagery associated with the action of war is lush, Babel's syntax is terse, compact, ascetically simple, so that his prose is a counterpoint of ornamental opulence and austere severity. The imagery plunges us into a world of high drama; the phrasing suggests resolute action.[5] Every clause opens with a subject followed by a verb, usually active. Except for the participial phrase, "thundering . . ." (where the style characteristically expands to indicate a conclusion), the passage is without subordination. A panoramic view

grows out of a string of discrete images, each given equal weight.
This paratactic accumulation has about it the linear inevitability of
traditional epic narration. The predominance of active verbs in the
present tense, the repetitive drumming of subject followed by verb,
the compact phrasing form an extremely assertive style. Babel's epic
manner is aggressively masculine.[6]

The dynamism of the prose is heightened by images that animate
the scene. As in Russia's great medieval epic *The Song of Igor's
Campaign,* or romantic pseudo-epics like Gogol's *Taras Bulba,* natural things by metaphorically assuming human qualities become
participants in the movements of men: "an orange sun rolls along
the sky like a lopped-off head"; "the breeze plays"; the Volyn twists
its "arms." Nature and man blend into a single totality, as the
sunset flies over the heads of the warriors like military standards,
and the thundering clamor of men merges with the roaring of the
river's torrents.

Throughout the book richly colored landscapes, brilliant midday
suns, floral sunsets form the backdrop for heroic action: "We were
moving to meet the sunset. Its foaming rivers flowed along the
embroidered napkins of peasants' fields. The stillness turned pink."
"It was after two of an expansive July day. A rainbow web of heat
shimmered in the air. Beyond the hilltops glittered a holiday band
of uniforms and horses' manes, braided with ribbons." "They rode
side by side, in identical jackets and gleaming silver-striped trousers,
on tall chestnut horses. Raising a shout the troops moved after
them, and pale steel flashed in the ichor of the autumnal sun."
Proud military standards regularly accompany these resplendent
marches: "The standards of the sunset fly over our heads." "On gilt
staffs, bearing velvet tassels, magnificent standards fluttered in fiery
pillars of dust" (*I,* 61, 102, 139, 27, 102).

The vivid colors that clothe the Cossacks and the vigorous style
that catches their movements separate them from humdrum life.
Men without innerness or subjectivity, they inhabit a heroic universe
removed from common concerns. Formulaic epithets capture their
heroic largeness: "I beheld the masterful indifference of a Tatar Khan
and recognized the horsemanship of the celebrated Kniga, the head-
strong Pavlichenko, the captivating Savitsky." They stand aloof from
ordinary human misery: "To the soothing accompaniment of the
peasants' incoherent and desperate clamor, Zh. sought out that
gentle pulsing in the brain that portends clarity and energy of

thought. Feeling at length the right beat, he snatched the last peasant tear drop, snarled imperiously, and walked off to Headquarters." Unsullied by the squalid and ravaged towns they pass through, indifferent to the suffering of their victims, the heroes reflect in their personal appearance the rarefied atmosphere of their enclosed field of force. The grays of day-to-day existence do not touch them. A Cossack officer, a paragon of masculine beauty, is shown in colors like those of the richly colored sky; the recurrent image of a proudly phallic standard evokes his heroic stature: "I wondered at the beauty of his giant's body. He rose, the purple of his riding breeches, the crimson of his tilted cap, the decorations of his chest cleaving the hut as a standard cleaves the sky. A smell of scent and the cloyingly sweet freshness of soap emanated from him. His long legs were like young girls sheathed to the neck in gleaming boots" (*I*, 70, 37, 53).

Though the Cossacks elicit Babel's respect, they are not spared his ironies. We have observed how in the *skaz* tales he contrasts the pretensions of their speech with the brutality of their natures. His heroes are beautiful, but also theatrical. They are partly observed individuals, partly, like the mobsters of the Moldavanka, products of a hyperbolic literary imagination. Lyutov's admiration for them is sincere, his sexual envy painful, but they smack too much of adolescent daydreams. The ironies create a tension in the image: blown up to mythic proportions, the Cossacks are simultaneously deflated downwards toward comic travesty.[7] In "Nachalnik konzapasa" (The remount officer) Dyakov, a former circus athlete, convinces complaining peasants that the nags they have been given in exchange for their requisitioned horses are serviceable. Dyakov's philosophy of horsemanship is elegantly simple: "If a horse falls and gets up, then it's a horse; if, to put it the other way round, it doesn't get up, then it's not a horse." Dyakov rides into the book as if he were an extra in an opera: "He skillfully swung his well-proportioned athlete's body out of the saddle. Straightening his splendid legs, . . . magnificent and agile, he moved toward the expiring animal, as if he were on stage. Dolefully it fixed its stubborn deep eyes on Dyakov and licked some imperceptible command from his ruddy palm. Immediately the exhausted horse felt a dextrous strength flowing from this gray-haired, vigorous, and dashing Romeo."

Individual Cossacks may be subjected to this type of aesthetic play, "a baring of the device" by which Babel, in Shklovsky's words, "places a heading over his portraits—opera."[8] Their march, however, is always solemn. It is also aimless. As in Tolstoy's *War and Peace,* history is made by men who have no idea what they are making. The Cossacks, not without codes of honor and principles of justice, are yet creatures of impulse. Revolution appeals to them by the opportunity it gives for free exercise of their powers, which they manifest in indiscriminate violence and mindless vengeance. The consciousness of the heroes of *Red Cavalry,* like the prose that conveys their progress, is riveted to the immediate present, the act of the moment, the event as pure event. Consequently, they are children of nature and their march, which is the march of history, is a kind of natural occurrence. Nature is necessity, something given and not made, the weather we live in rather than forms we create. Natural things exhibit motion, whereas humans are capable of action—motions that result from deliberate choice. From the opening passage, where physical nature and human activity merge in a single awesome march, the movement of armies is presented as a spontaneous and ineluctable force, an elemental "Cossack flood" (*I,* 43).

Standing on a border line between nature and culture, part god, part man, part savage, the warrior is threatened by emptiness: "The brilliant sky loomed inexpressibly empty, as it always is in times of danger." Besides the regal standard, another recurring image for war is the desert or wasteland (*pustynya*): "Afonka dragged himself to his squadron, utterly alone, in the blazing desert of the fields." "Beyond the windows horses neighed and Cossacks shouted. The desert of war yawned beyond the window." In the desert of war men suffer "an eternal homelessness." Some turn into beasts. Matvey Pavlichenko has a "jackal's conscience" and was "suckled by a she-wolf"; Afonka Bida roams the countryside slaughtering Poles like a "lonely wolf." When life is reduced to pure motion, empty of reflection and conscious purpose, barren of the nurture and restraints of culture, men turn into wild animals, or they feel themselves "utterly alone" (*I,* 104, 59, 107, 80, 105). The man without a city, Aristotle tells us, becomes either a god or a beast.[9] What escapes him is the specifically human.

Pathos

"Crossing into Poland," with which we began our discussion of the epic and pathetic modes, is in its structure exemplary of most of the stories that make up *Red Cavalry*. The first half of its brief two pages, devoted to the resplendent march of the Cossack army, is more a prose poem than short story. After the baroque overture, the narrative proper begins, breaking the story, in a way characteristic of Babel, in two. The presentation shifts from the collective "we" of the epic march to the personal "I" of the narrator's story. Lyutov is billeted in a Jewish hovel, goes to sleep, dreams dreams of violence, and is awakened by a pregnant woman, who tells him he has been sleeping next to the corpse of her father. In sharp contrast to the glorious march, the Jewish dwelling is described in sordidly naturalistic detail: "In the room I was given I discovered wardrobes in disarray, scraps of women's fur coats on the floor, human feces, fragments of occult crockery. . . ." The Jews who live in this filth are grotesquely deformed victims of poverty and violence: "They skip about noiselessly, like monkeys, like Japs in a circus, their necks swaying and twisting. . . . The dead old man lies there, thrown on his back. His throat has been torn out, his face ripped in two, blue blood clots his beard like a lump of lead."

Heroic beauty and power are contrasted with the ugliness of suffering. But the story does not end here. In a concluding coda the pregnant Jewess bursts into an impassioned speech: " 'Sir, . . . the Poles cut his throat, and he begging them: Kill me in the backyard so that my daughter won't see me die. But they did as suited them. He died in this room, thinking of me. And now I'd like to know,' the woman cried out with sudden and terrible power, 'I'd like to know where in the world you could find another father like my father?' " The epic mode, for all its vigorous insistence, does not displace the pathetic. They make rival claims on the imagination. Competing with the Cossack power of action is "the terrible power" of human suffering, in particular, Jewish suffering, "a power full of somber greatness" (*I,* 64).

The contrasting parts are integral miniatures. Until the conclusion, which reveals a heroic dignity hidden beneath the squalid surface of the Jewish hovel, there is no attempt to bridge the two sections. The narrative is perfunctory—Lyutov visits the Jewish

home solely that we may see it. For the expansiveness of narrative
Babel substitutes rhapsodic rhetoric and an intense lyric concentration upon images. His story does not move to the denouement of
an action but to an epiphany.

"Crossing into Poland" veers from the action of war to life on
the wayside, from poetic description to a sketchy narrative. "Kostel
v Novograde" (The church at Novograd) follows an analogous procedure, except that scenes of culture become the object of poetic
evocation and the business of war constitutes the narrative. Lyutov
goes to report to an army commissar who has been billeted in the
Catholic church of the title. The church, the adjacent priest's house,
and their denizens are described. Then the story proper begins, as
the commissar arrives with a squad of Cossacks, who search the
church where they uncover concealed money and valuables.

The church is depicted in the languid style and hothouse imagery
of fin de siècle decadence. It is a place of ruin, putrefaction, and
silky perversity: "The breath of an invisible order flickered under
the ruins of the priest's house, and its insinuating seductions un-
manned me. Oh crucifixes, tiny as the talismans of courtesans,
parchment of Papal Bulls and satin of women's letters, rotting in
the blue silk of waistcoats! . . . I see the wounds of your god,
oozing seed, a fragrant poison intoxicating virgins. . . . Beyond
the window the garden path shimmered beneath the black passion
of the sky. Thirsty roses swayed in the darkness. Flashes of green
lightning flamed amid the cupolas. A naked corpse sprawled along
the slope. The moonlight streamed over lifeless legs thrust apart.
Here is Poland, here is the proud sorrow of the Res Publica!" The
heroic march pulses with vitality; places of culture are frozen in
immobility. The verbs, mostly intransitive, many reflexive (*mertsalo,
perlivaetsya, kolyshutsya, pylayut, valyaetsya, struitsya*), describe motions fixed in place. Where the verbs capturing the epic march place
events in time—"a tender light flares," "we ford the river," "the
horses enter the water"—these convey states of objects. Their length,
the open syllables, and profusion of liquids (*vkradchivye ego soblazny
obessilili menya*) slow the tempo and contribute to the "insinuating"
quality. Interspersed through the passage are verbless exclamations
("Oh crucifixes") that show the passage for what it is—a static
evocation of a world: "Here is Poland . . . !"

Jewish places also languish in stasis. They are pictured, as in
"Crossing into Poland," in inert catalogs of useless things—broken

crockery, scraps of fur, feces—or in a highly evocative manner like that employed for the church at Novograd. "Kladbishche v Kozine" (The cemetery at Kozin) is a short prose poem. Almost verbless, it is an incantation, singing through the inscriptions on the gravestones of a dead world surviving only as memory.

> Azrael son of Ananias, lips of Jehovah.
> Elijah son of Azrael, a mind waging lonely battle with oblivion.
> Wolff son of Elijah, prince robbed from the Torah in his nineteenth spring.
> Judah son of Wolff, Rabbi of Kraków and Prague.
> O death, O covetous one, O greedy thief, why couldst thou not have spared us, just for once?

In the second half of "The Church at Novograd," the narrative half devoted to the search, the short, clipped accents of Babel's military style assert themselves: "My Commissar still hasn't shown up. I look for him in the Staff, the garden, the church. . . . We make our rounds, searching [*kruzhimsya i ishchem*]. . . ."

As "Crossing into Poland" opposed Cossack vigor and Jewish suffering, "The Church at Novograd" parallels Catholic mystery and the brusque business of revolution and war. Babel's almost plotless sketches required an ordering principle which he found in contrast. The contrast, which may initially seem schematic, is then complicated. Suffering is ugly and yet has about it an awesome dignity. The decadent charms of Catholicism are "unmanning" and yet "seductive." At the conclusion Lyutov rejects its feminized culture ("crucifixes tiny as the talismans of courtesans, parchment of Papal Bulls and satin of women's letters") to rejoin the world of masculine action: "Away from these winking madonnas deceived by common soldiers!" Nevertheless the mysteries of culture continue to lure his imagination.

"Berestechko" combines all three social groupings—Catholic Poland, the Jewish Pale, and the revolutionary army. The pattern of presentation is the same. We are now in the middle of the book, war has muted the songs and darkened the colors of the Cossack march, but it still beats with power: "We were on the march from Khotin to Berestechko. The fighting men dozed in their tall saddles. A song gurgled like a brook running dry. Monstrous corpses lay upon thousand-year-old burial mounds. . . . Divisional Commander Pavlichenko's cloak flew over the Staff like a somber flag. . . . We rode past the Cossack burial mounds, past Bogdan Khmelnitsky's watchtower. An old man with a bandura crept out from behind a gravestone and in a child's voice sang of ancient Cossack glory. We listened to his song in silence and to the sounds of a thundering march burst into Berestechko."

Lyutov wanders into the Jewish quarter, a cramped and sunless ghetto. Excrement, useless waste, is a recurring detail in descriptions of Jewish habitats: "The sun never penetrates here. . . . In wartime the inhabitants seek refuge from bullets and pillage in these catacombs. Human offal and cow dung accumulate here for days. Depression and horror fill the catacombs with the corrosive and foul acidity of excrement."

Depressed by Jewish misery, Lyutov walks off to the deserted castle of a Polish aristocrat, where Gothic moonlight supplants the brilliant sunlight of battle, sinister green hues and watery shades displace the regal purple and bright red, orange, and yellow of the heroic landscape: "The moon, green as a lizard, rose above the pond. From my window I could make out the estate of the Counts Raciborski—meadows and hopfields, hidden by the watery ribbons of twilight." The Raciborski family history is a tale of decay, of a mad ninety-year-old countess, her impotent son, and a "dying family line." A yellowing letter dated 1820 announces the birth of a child and recalls a time when the Raciborskis, still fruitful, could look to the future. In the distance a commissar is heard making a speech.

Lyutov feels the pull of two forces—the commissar's imperious rhetoric and the insinuating seductions of the old order. Building his stories on contrast, Babel is also fond of contrasting syntax, of coordinate sentences whose clauses clash: "He spoke of the Second Congress of the Comintern, while I wandered past walls where nymphs with gouged out eyes were leading an ancient choral dance." Aristocratic culture, though impotent and doomed, still exerts the fascination of art. The story concludes on the notes of power which opened it. "You are in power," the commissar exhorts. "Everything here is yours. There are no more Pans. I now proceed to the election of the Revolutionary Committee." Lyutov ambles in a no-man's land, recognizing the unequivocal voice of power, drawn to the sinuous paths of culture and the pathos of dying ways.

Apocalypse

The epic line persists through the book, but its colors gradually darken. By the time of "Berestechko," a little over halfway through, the standard of the sunset has become a "somber flag"; the thundering songs now gurgle "like a brook running dry"; silent Cossacks ride by monstrous corpses. Toward the end, in "Zamoste," the landscape of war turns nightmarish: "Rain fell. Over the flooded earth flew wind and darkness. The stars were blotted out by ink-swollen clouds. . . . The raw dawn flowed over us like waves of chloroform. Green rockets soared above the Polish camp. . . . More rain fell. Dead mice floated along the roads. Autumn set its ambushes about our hearts, and trees like naked corpses set upright on their feet swayed at the crossroads." The imagery accumulates until it forms an apocalyptic vision of the death of things. The story follows the usual pattern, shifting from an extended portrait to specific incidents. However, instead of furnishing contrast now, an encounter with a peasant merely adds to the sense of a world engulfed in total violence.

The peasant made me light a cigarette from his. "The Jews are to blame for everything, on our side and yours. There'll be mighty few of them left after the war. How many Jews are there in the whole world?"

"Ten million," I answered.

"There'll be only two hundred thousand left," cried the peasant, and touched my hand, afraid I would go.

Much of *Red Cavalry* has a fantastical, at times even hallucinatory quality—moonlit Gothic churches, green skies hovering over deserted manors. "Zamoste" alternates between a reality turned nightmare and a dream of escape. Caught up in a maelstrom of destruction, Lyutov, seeking the embrace of the maternal earth, dreams of comfort at a woman's breast. However, to turn back in nostalgia to the mother is also a kind of death:

The sodden ground offered me the soothing embrace of the tomb. . . . I dreamed of a shed all carpeted with hay. . . . a woman dressed as for a ball came over to me. She freed her breast from the black lace of her bodice and raised it to me, carefully, like a nurse proffering food. She laid

her breast against mine. An aching warmth stirred in the depths of my
soul, and drops of sweat—live, stirring sweat—seethed between our nipples.

"Margot," I longed to cry out, "the earth is dragging me like a jibbering
cur by the cord of its calamities. Nevertheless I have seen you, Margot."

. . . "Jesus," she said, "receive the soul of thy departed servant."

She placed two worn five-kopeck pieces on my eyelids, and stuffed the
orifice of my mouth with fragrant hay. My moaning vainly beat about
inside my clamped jaws, my failing pupils turned slowly beneath the
copper coins, I could not force my hands apart. . . .

Upon awakening, he rejoins the violence. The story concludes in
bitter irony: "Silence. 'We've lost the campaign,' muttered Volkov,
and snored. 'Yes,' I answered."

Whichever way Lyutov turns, he comes up against unsatisfactory
choices, incomplete versions of the self he is struggling to shape.
Heroic action and masculine power are compelling, but too often
they manifest themselves as hollow theatrical gesture or purposeless
cruelty. Violence, understood broadly, is an essential ingredient of
creativity: the artist does violence to the language he has inherited,
the revolutionist to the social order he lives in. But violence in *Red
Cavalry* is always on the edge of becoming an end in itself, barbarism
loosed from the humanizing restraints of culture. In its darker moments, as in "Zamoste," Lyutov is the witness, not of a painful
birth, but of a cataclysm of death. To retreat to dreams of maternal
comfort is to die as a man. The worlds of culture offer the solace
of art and the nourishment of community, but these too are dying.

The Jews

The double pull of the book—its alternation between attraction
and repulsion—is perhaps strongest in the sections devoted to Lyutov's fellow Jews. Gedali, protagonist of the story bearing his name,
is the aged and blind proprietor of a curiosity shop, a museum of
dead objects: "Here before me is the market and the death of the
market. The fat soul of plenty is dead. Dumb padlocks hang upon
the booths, and the granite pavement is as clean as the bald pate
of a corpse. . . . There were buttons and a dead butterfly. . . .
[Gedali] wound in and out of a labyrinth of globes, skulls, and dead
flowers, waving a many colored feather duster of cock's plumes and
blowing dust from the dead flowers. . . . A vague odor of corruption enfolded me."

Surrounded by death, Gedali, in green frock coat sweeping to the ground and top hat resembling a black tower, is yet a prophet of life. His eyes have been closed by Polish anti-Semites, but his ears are attuned to mysterious voices wafting in the night air. (Armies clash in brilliant sunlight; the cultures of the wayside are shrouded in twilight or night.) Gedali's prophetic dreams are of the final "sweet revolution" of joy, of an "International of Good People," who see to it that there are no orphans in the house and that every soul receives "first-category rations." To Gedali's Messianic Revolution, the narrator answers with the voice of the actual historical Revolution, in clipped accents of violence and power: "The sunlight doesn't enter eyes that are closed. But we will cut open those closed eyes."

Lyutov, however, cannot maintain his aggressive posture. The story had begun in tones of elegiac lyricism and prayerlike incantation, Babel's other way (in addition to naturalistic portraiture) of evoking Jewish places: "On Sabbath eves I am oppressed by the dense melancholy of memories. In bygone days on these evenings my grandfather would stroke with his yellow beard the tomes of Ibn-Ezra. . . . On these evenings my child's heart rocked like a little ship on enchanted waves. O the rotted Talmuds of my childhood! O the dense melancholy of memories! I roam Zhitomir in search of a timid star. . . ." When at the end of the story the Sabbath star rises out of the blue darkness to assume her throne, Lyutov softens. Throughout *Red Cavalry* the sharing of food is a token of comradeship and community. "Gedali" concludes in an ironic reversal of its initial contrasts. The Revolution has energy but offers poor nourishment to the starved souls of men; Lyutov, who had asserted its vitality, turns for nourishment to the dead world of Gedali.

"Pan comrade, you don't know what the International is eaten with."

"It is eaten with gunpowder and spiced with best-quality blood."

And then, from out of the blue dark, the young Sabbath ascended to her throne.

"Gedali," I said, "today is Friday, and it's already evening. Where are Jewish cakes to be got, and a Jewish glass of tea, and a bit of that pensioned-off God in a glass of tea?"

The stories we have examined reveal the paradoxical structure of *Red Cavalry*. Built around contrast, they oppose the epic march of revolution to the suffering of the old order. The former is described in a style of energy, movement, and color; the latter is pictured in images of decay and death and in a style suggesting stasis. But if the epic line of the book is vibrant and forceful, it is also barren— a desert of the heart. The old ways are rotting but it is among them that Lyutov seeks sustenance. In Catholic Poland he feels the lure of art and the pathos of a vanished culture; among his fellow Jews, he experiences nostalgia for familial traditions and the pathos of suffering.

Culture

Culture for Babel is a mysterious thing. It belongs to night, the moon, and the lonely Sabbath star as opposed to the sunlight of clamorous events. The shifts from the clear sunlight and martial rhythms of the epic to the mysterious moonlit nights and evocative language of the pathetic mode mark a change in kinds of experience. Language and imagery combine to determine the book's shape of feeling. In the daylight of the epic-heroic world, in the arena of history, action is precise, unreflective, and violent. Life admits of clearcut categorization, as humanity divides into agent and patient, actor and sufferer, forger of the future and remnant of the dying past. But in the realm of human culture, where man gives himself to creation and thought, everything is hopelessly ambiguous: "I went along with the moon, nursing unrealizable dreams and discordant songs" (*I*, 45).

The figures representing culture in *Red Cavalry* embody its mysteries and paradoxes. They are incongruous, slightly comic, yet inspired: "Old Gedali, the diminutive proprietor in smoked glasses and a green frock coat down to the ground, meandered around his treasures in the roseate void of evening. He rubbed his small white hands, plucked his little grey beard, and listened, head bent, to the mysterious voices wafting down to him" (*I*, 50). His Gentile counterpart is the Polish artist Pan Apolek, of the story bearing his name, who is also a child of the evening: "On fragrant evenings the shades of old feudal Poland assembled, the mad [*yurodivy*] artist at their head." Like Gedali, he has a touch of the whimsical about him: "In his right hand Apolek carried a paintbox, and with his left he guided the blind accordian player. The singing of their nailed German boots rang out with peace and hope. From Apolek's thin neck dangled a canary-yellow scarf. Three little chocolate-colored feathers fluttered on the blind man's Tyrolean hat. . . . It looked as though . . . the Muses had settled at the organ side by side in bright, wadded scarves and hobnailed German boots."

Incongruous in appearance, Apolek leads a life and pursues an art that are exercises in paradox. He is at one and the same time a decorator of Christian churches and a heretic. His favorite story is the apocryphal tale of Jesus lying out of pity with the virgin Deborah. His art carries "a portent of mystery," the mystery of the ways the ordinary can be transformed by art. Apolek spends his life raising the poor and sinful to the condition of saints in icons of glorious color. "He has made saints of you in your lifetime," the indignant church authorities complain.

Apolek's artistic vision is but a variant of the Hasid Gedali's prophetic dream of the coming Revolution of Joy and the International of Good People. Polish village artist and Jewish shopkeeper represent the aesthetic and ethical imaginations, respectively. Engulfed by violence, both cling to dreams of universal compassion. And as in his encounter with Gedali, Lyutov softens in Apolek's presence: "I then made a vow to follow Pan Apolek's example. And the sweetness of a dreamer's malice, my bitter scorn for the curs and swine of mankind, the flame of silent and intoxicating revenge—all this I sacrificed to my new vow."

Even the Cossacks have a visionary bard: Sashka, of "Sashka Khristos" (Sashka the Christ). The tale opens in tones of legend: "Sashka was his name, and he was called Christ on account of his gentleness." This homely hagiography recounts Sashka's passage from a state of sin to sanctity. Away from the heroic march we get glimpses of a Cossack society that is coarse and brutish. In keeping with his mean subject matter Babel tells Sashka's story in a colloquial manner, with much of the speech in dialect. Lyutov's voice momentarily dissolves into the language of the depicted milieu to form a kind of *skaz*.

Sashka is fourteen when his stepfather Tarakanych (the name means cockroach) introduces him to the pleasures of sex through a crippled beggar. They contract a venereal disease, which does not stop the stepfather from intercourse with the boy's mother. As they return from this sexual adventure they pass through a natural world as lovely as the human is ugly. Descriptions of nature in Babel's fiction strive for lyrical expressiveness and metaphorical nuance rather

than mimetic exactitude. Built upon formulas, they tend toward
abstraction: poppies are crimson, rye is yellow, fog is pearly. However, the imaginativeness of metaphor saves his prose from cliché:
"The earth lay in April dampness. In the black hollows emeralds
glistened. Green shoots embroidered the earth in intricate stitches."

Sashka soon has enough of Tarakanych's cruelties and asks his
permission to follow the ways of the saints and become a shepherd.
It would be tempting to say that Sashka has been inspired to take
this decision by the beauties of nature, but Babel does not probe
the psychology of his characters. Symbolic and poetic vision replaces
rational motivation: "The force of his vision held him spellbound.
Surrendering to it he rejoiced in his daydream. It seemed to him
that two silver cords . . . were suspended from the sky, and attached
to them a cradle—a cradle of rosewood with a floral pattern. It
swung high above the earth and far from the skies, and the silver
cords swayed and sparkled. Sashka lay in the cradle, and the air
wafted over him. The air, resonant as music, blew from the fields,
and a rainbow blossomed over the unripe corn. Sashka rejoiced in
his day dream. . . ."

Sashka heeds the music of his dreams and becomes the village
holy man, "Sashka the Christ." Like Gedali and Pan Apolek, he
follows a private vision that sets him apart from the common run.
He is a gentle child thrown among brutal men. His gentleness may
have something to do with his disease; the failed and the hurt seek
him out "for his love and his illness." He is also, like Apolek, an
artist of sorts, a singer. In battle the Cossacks protect him because
men "need songs" (*I, 147*).

In many of the stories of *Red Cavalry* the narrator initially relin-
quishes his role as character only to resume it at the end. Momentarily granted the status of objective narration, the tale is then
converted into food for the narrator's reflections. At the conclusion
Sashka's story also becomes Lyutov's, as the sophisticated intellectual
discovers in the simple boy a kindred spirit: "I got to know Sashka
the Christ. . . . Since then we have often met the dawn and seen
the sun set together. And whenever the capricious chance of war
has brought us together, we have sat down of an evening on the
bench outside a hut, or made tea in the woods in a sooty kettle, or
slept side by side in the new-mown fields, the hungry horses tied
to his foot or mine."

Grieved by the barbarism of war, Lyutov turns to the paths of culture for solace. He has no illusions about social institutions, which are crumbling under the impact of Revolution. Instead he is attracted to lonely and eccentric men who represent culture's ultimate values. Pan Apolek and Sashka the Christ are artists—one a painter, the other a singer: in time of war men need songs. Gedali is a man of faith, steeped in old familial and communal traditions, who has not forgotten the joy of a Jewish cup of tea. Above all, Jewish Hasidic prophet, heretical Polish painter, and village singer and saint share a capacity for compassion.

As action is the measure of man in the heroic-epic world, so compassion is a cardinal value of culture. It provides the nourishment missing from the deserts of war. Night, which shrouds Catholic churches, Polish estates, and Jewish villages, is a time of comfort. While the images of day are masculine—phallic standards cleaving brilliant sunlit skies—those of night are maternal: "Blue roads flowed past me like streams of milk spurting from many breasts"; "evening wrapped me in the life-giving moisture of its twilight sheets, evening laid a mother's hand upon my burning forehead"; "night comforted us in our sorrows, a light wind wafted over us like a mother's skirt." Gedali exalts the figure of the compassionate mother to a metaphysical principle: "All is mortal. Only the mother is destined for eternal life. And when the mother is no longer among the living, she leaves a memory which no one has yet dared to defile. The memory of the mother nourishes in us a compassion that is like the ocean. The measureless ocean nourishes the rivers that dissect the universe. . . . In the passionate edifice of Hasidism the windows and doors have been knocked out, but it is immortal, like the soul of the mother. With oozing eye sockets Hasidism still stands at the crossroads of the winds of history" (*I*, 46, 56, 99, 57).

Initiation

To become fully a man Lyutov must give up the mother. In "Moy pervy gus" (My first goose) he is assigned to Commander Savitsky's division. Confronted by this ideal of manly beauty, he is filled with awe and envy. Derision greets him: "Guys with specs are a drag here. . . . It's no life for high falutin types. But you go and mess up a lady, a real clean one too, and you'll have the boys patting you on the back." Lyutov performs the rape symbolically, by killing the goose of a landlady who had refused to feed him. The act is like a pagan rite of initiation: "The Cossacks in the yard were already sitting around their cauldron. They sat motionless, erect, like heathen priests at a sacrifice. . . ." The results are mixed. In despair at his rejection, Lyutov had sought escape in reading from Lenin, but "the beloved lines came toward me along a thorny path and could not reach me." After the ritual murder he is accepted by the Cossacks and reads to them. He feels the joy of manly camaraderie, and touches a masculine principle: "I read on and exulted, and in my exultation caught the secret curve of Lenin's straight line." But he suffers from guilt. Babel's choice of words points to an identification with the victim that is at the root of Lyutov's conflict: as the goose's head "cracked and oozed" (*tresnula i potekla*), Lyutov's heart, "stained with bloodshed, grated and brimmed over" (*skripelo i teklo*). Overcome by guilt, he longs for maternal comfort: "Evening wrapped about me the life-giving moisture of its twilight sheets, evening laid a mother's hand upon my burning forehead. . . . We slept, all six of us, beneath a torn roof that let in the stars, warming one another, our legs intertwined. I dreamed and in my dreams saw women. But my heart, stained with bloodshed, grated and brimmed over."

Lyutov's conflict admits of no easy solution. To choose Gedali's way, the way of the "compassionate mother," is to deny the imperatives of action and also, in the entanglements of war, even to deny compassion. In "Smert Dolgushova" (The death of Dolgushov) the wounded Dolgushov implores Lyutov to finish him off so as to save him from torture at the hands of the Poles. The Cossacks interpret his inability to fulfill the request as a failure of pity: "You guys in specs have about as much pity for us fellows as a cat for a mouse." It is the terrible irony of war that to assume manly responsibility one must learn to kill. In "Posle boya" (After the battle) Lyutov is ashamed when the Cossacks discover that he has gone into battle with an unloaded gun. Taunted as a religious pacifist (*molokan*), he walks off into the night imploring fate to grant him "the simplest of proficiencies—the ability to kill my fellowmen." Violence fills him with guilt, but to stay with the mother is a violence committed upon the self, a denial of one's manly nature. As in "Zamoste," where the dream of a nourishing woman is associated with the hero's death, in "After the Battle" night, the time of maternal comfort, is revealed as a time of martyrdom: "Evening

flew up to the sky like a flock of birds, and darkness crowned me
with its watery wreath. I felt my strength ebbing away. Bent beneath
a funereal garland, I walked on. . . ."

Resolution

Isaac Babel's great book continually circles a tragic dilemma. The
march of history will not be denied, but it leaves men spiritually
famished. The cultures—artistic, religious, moral—which nourish
human life are dying. To linger nostalgically in an irretrievable past
is to die oneself. The forward march of history and the preservative
patterns of culture are never brought into harmony, but the final
two stories—"Syn rabbi" (The rabbi's son) and "Argamak"—do
seek out a middle ground.

The rebellious rabbi's son appears in an earlier sketch, "Rabbi,"
as "the cursed son, the last son, the recalcitrant son." By the end
of *Red Cavalry* this last son of the rabbi's line has joined the Red
Army, taken command of a regiment, and been mortally wounded.
Like Gedali and Pan Apolek, Ilya is a paradoxical figure. His description combines both male and female features: "a youth . . .
with the powerful brow of Spinoza, with the sickly face of a nun."
While going through the dying Ilya's belongings, Lyutov discovers
that he has lugged off to war emblems of all the opposites of the
book: action and poetry, politics and art, things masculine and
feminine: "Everything was strewn about pell-mell—mandates of
the propagandist and notes of the Jewish poet. The portraits of
Lenin and Maimonides lay side by side, the knotted iron of Lenin's
skull beside the dull silk of the portraits of Maimonides. A lock of
woman's hair had been slipped into a volume of Resolutions of the
Sixth Party Congress, and curved lines of Hebrew verse crowded
the margins of Communist leaflets. They fell on me in a sparse and
mournful rain—pages of the Song of Songs and revolver cartridges."

Ilya has found a way, not to reconcile the contradictions of existence, but to live with them. When he goes off to war, he takes
the baggage of culture with him. The tokens of culture lie side by
side with those of revolution and war, but they remain antagonistic
to the end. A mood of elegiac melancholy sweeps over Lyutov as
he once again stands face to face with the tragic incongruity of
human life.

That mood is not one in which he or the rabbi's son will permit himself to linger. Explaining to Lyutov why he went off to war, Ilya says that, though formerly he would not abandon his mother, in a revolution a mother is only "an episode." She is also "an episode" for Lyutov. In the course of the book he struggles against the webs of nostalgia that tie him to the mother, and in the final story, "Argamak," he breaks free to join the epic march of the Cossack army. He passes the test of mastering a horse—the sine qua non of Cossack manliness—and the Cossacks finally accept him: "I realized my dream. The Cossacks stopped watching me and my horse."

The maternal image and related images of nurturing have been associated with culture and value. The mother, source of life and center of the family, provides the continuity culture demands. But in *Red Cavalry* culture is also "episodic." The structures in which men and women live—family, nation, religion, and tradition— appear to have a permanence that the juggernaut of history belies. Lyutov rejects the temptations of nostalgia to accept, stoically, the exigencies of history.

However, culture is ultimately not an institution but an idea, and even as its institutions crumble in revolution, its idea is kept alive. For Gedali, the mother, even when dead, "leaves a memory" which is "immortal." It is surely no accident that the representative figures of culture in *Red Cavalry*, Gedali and Pan Apolek, are marginal men—Jewish mystic and Catholic heretic. Less tied than others to temporal institutions and orthodoxies, they remain loyal to visions of compassion in the midst of a crumbling world. Gedali is confident that his values, if not yet realized as actualities, will survive as memories at the "crossroads of history."

At the end the rabbi's son joins these two to become the most important of the work's bearers of culture. As Apolek offered a model of the artist to Lyutov—"I vowed . . . to follow the example of Pan Apolek"—the rabbi's son gives him a model of action. Lyutov feels a kinship with him stronger than any he has known before: "And I—scarcely containing the tempests of my imagination in my ancient body—I received the last breath of my brother." Lyutov joins the Cossacks, but he is too much a man of culture to go completely native. Gedali and Pan Apolek attract him by their commitment to ethical and aesthetic values, but they are dreamers and visionaries, too remote from the realities of history to teach him how to live in the world. The rabbi's son shows him a middle course between mindless violence and Messianic imaginings. While participating in the violence, which he deems necessary, he also keeps alive reminders of other ways: poetry, the thought of Maimonides, a lock of woman's hair. In choosing masculine action, he refuses to deny the feminine part of his nature. He decides to live with the contradictions of culture and force.

The Cossack army Lyutov joins at the end of *Red Cavalry* is not the army that burst into the book in a blaze of color at the start. It now bears the scars of war. From the "standards of the sunset" of "Crossing into Poland" through the "somber flag" of Berestechko and the deathly scenes of "Zamoste" the fields of war undergo a progressive darkening. Babel starts out with a romantically charged picture of war, then brings us close to its brutal actuality. The cumulative violence has a numbing effect on Lyutov, who for a time dreams of escape in the warm womb of the earth before resolving to ride with the horses of war. In the meantime the Cossacks have moved from the condition of glorious beasts or gods to that of wounded men. As they cross the line separating the poetic idealization of the epic-heroic mode from the grim naturalism of the pathetic, they have begun to resemble their victims. A Cossack warrior, Tikhomolov,

came wearing galoshes on his bare feet. His fingers had been chopped up, and ribbons of black lint hung down from them, dragging after him like a cloak. . . . Baulin was sitting on the steps of the church, steaming his feet in a tub. His feet were putrescent. . . . Tufts of youthful straw stuck to Baulin's forehead. The sun blazed on the bricks and tiles of the church. . . . Tikhomolov, dragging his mantle of rags, went over to the horses, his galoshes squelching. Argamak stretched out his long neck and neighed toward his master, neighed in a soft squeal, like a horse in the desert. On his back the inflamed lymph twisted lacelike between the strips of torn flesh. Tikhomolov stood next to the horse. The filthy ribbons of bandage trailed unstirring on the ground. (*I*, 155)[10]

Ultimately, Cossack, Jew, and Pole are united in suffering.

The unblinking acceptance of tragedy makes *Red Cavalry* a great book. Babel rigorously eschews didacticism or the sentimentalism of synthetic reconciliation. He does not have a lesson to teach but a world to show. His book is imperfect. The prose, though moving and often lovely, sometimes slips into pyrotechnic virtuosity. His

Cossacks, if not for his qualifying ironies, would be mere projections of adolescent daydreams. Yet in the long run Babel is not a writer to delude himself. He keeps a hard, cold eye on experience. For a world torn by the rival claims of culture and power, compassion and violence, he finds no comfortable solution. He stands with the rabbi's son, in stoic determination to live with ambiguity. The resolution of *Red Cavalry* does not lie in the triumph of any single allegiance, but in an assertion of the will to live in a discordant world.[11]

Chapter Seven

Disorder and Early Sorrow:
The Story of My Dovecot

Though two of the four stories that make up the *Dovecot* cycle were written in the year in which *Red Cavalry* was completed and the others five years later, they may in fact be read as a prologue to Babel's epic of the Civil War. Presented as autobiographical tales, they tell the story of a boy's struggle to escape the confinements of his home and culture and enter the wide world, or how Isaac Babel grew up to be Kirill Lyutov.

As in *Red Cavalry,* each story stands on its own but the whole is still tied together by the thread of a continuous plot. The boy's successive ages indicate Babel had a progressive development in mind, and it is regrettable that editors have not seen fit to publish the stories in series. At the opening of the first he is nine, in the second ten, twelve in the third, and fourteen in the last. The first three bring him to the verge of breaking away, and in each he suffers a traumatic experience. In the cycle's title story, "Istoriya moey golubyatni" (The story of my dovecot, 1925), and in "Pervaya lyubov" (First love, 1925) disappointment in his father causes much of his pain; in "V podvale" (In the basement, 1931) other male relations are responsible for his humiliation. By the time of "Pro-buzhdenie" (Awakening, 1932) he has had enough of the whole mess and is ready, and soon will be old enough, for flight.

"The Story of My Dovecot"

"The Story of My Dovecot" opens in 1904, a year before the revolution of 1905 and the pogroms that accompanied it. The scene is the town of Nikolaev (not far from Odessa), where the Babels lived at the time. The quota for admission to the local secondary school or gymnasium was tight—a mere 5 percent—and Jewish children were subject to excruciating examination. To inspire his young charge, the boy's ambitious father has promised to buy him pigeons, in return demanding no less than the Russian equivalent of A plusses. His son is bright: "The teachers, though they employed cunning, could not rob me of my intelligence and avid memory." He takes the oral examination in a state of hysteria—"a long childish dream of despair"—a condition that frequently assaults this nervous, frail child in the course of the four stories. He gets his A plusses, but his triumph is shortlived. A wealthy Jewish merchant bribes an official to improve the odds for his own child, and his grades are lowered. He repeats his ordeal a year later, again in a hysterical fit of fear mixed with the exhilarating freedom of one losing control of himself: "About Peter the Great I knew things by heart from Putsykovich's book and Pushkin's verses. Sobbing I recited these verses. . . . trembling, throwing myself erect, rushing headlong, I was shouting Pushkin's stanzas at the top of my voice. On and on I yelled them, and no one broke into my crazy mouthings. Through a crimson blindness, through the sense of absolute freedom that had taken hold of me, I was aware of nothing but Pyatnitsky's ancient face with its silver-touched beard bent toward me. He didn't interrupt me, and merely said to Karavaev, who was rejoicing for my sake and Pushkin's: 'What a people, . . . these Jews of yours. . . .' "

The boy triumphs and his father celebrates. Members of a despised minority, his father's fellow salesmen, grain dealers, and brokers regard his victory as theirs: "In this toast the old man congratulated my parents and said that I had vanquished all my foes in single combat: I had vanquished the Russian boys with their fat cheeks, and I had vanquished the sons of our own vulgar parvenus. So too in ancient times David King of Judah had overcome Goliath, and just as I had triumphed over Goliath, so too would our people by the strength of their intellect conquer the foes who had encircled us and were thirsting for our blood." To be a David of the mind is no easy burden for a boy of nine. His mother, less innocent than his father, more cognizant of the uncontrollable accidents of life, is apprehensive: "My mother was pale; she was experiencing destiny through my eyes. She looked at me with bitter compassion as one might look at a little cripple, because she alone knew what a family ours was for misfortune."

For the men of his family circle the boy's achievement is representative, and hence abstract. Frustrated in their own lives, they rob him of his triumph by generalizing it into a triumph of the

Jewish people. The boy, on the other hand, views his achievement wholly in concrete terms. Passing the examination allows him to enjoy the simple pleasures of the smells of a new pencil box and books, and he shares these delights with his mother. Success promises him pigeons. In *Red Cavalry* Lyutov struggles to escape the hold of the mother; in the *Dovecot* cycle it is the father the boy must first flee, in a flight that takes him from life as abstraction to life as concrete experience, and also from dependent conformity to the freedom of creativity. In the meantime the boy turns to his mother (and other maternal figures) for intimacy and stability in a culture where men without power live in dreams.

The mother's anxiety over the vagaries of fate turns out to be well founded, for the boy has the bad luck to win his trophy at the moment of an anti-Semitic riot. First he hears of his beloved granduncle's murder; then a crippled pedlar, furious at his inability to scurry about for loot, squashes one of his prize pigeons against his face. History has caught up with young Babel. From the cramped but protective confines of home and ghetto he has moved into a universe of contingency, where individual hopes and ambitions mean little. In his pain he has a vision that echoes the central images of *Red Cavalry*. Great horses stride through space, misfortune on their backs. The moist earth offers comfort. It is a source of life and yet a tomb of death. It is as if Babel the boy anticipates his future as Lyutov the man, while Babel the writer is still haunted by the images of his earlier book.

I lay on the ground, and the guts of the crushed bird trickled down my temple. They flowed down my cheek, winding this way and that, splashing, blinding me. The tender blue guts slid down over my forehead, and I closed my solitary unstopped eye so as not to see the world that spread out before me. . . . My world was tiny, and it was awful. I closed my eyes so as not to see it, and pressed myself to the ground that lay beneath me in soothing muteness. This trampled earth in no way resembled our life, waiting for exams in our life. Somewhere far away Woe rode across it on a great steed, but the noise of the hoofbeats grew weaker and died away, and silence, the bitter silence that sometimes overwhelms children in their sorrow, suddenly annihilated the boundary between my body and the immobile earth. The earth smelled of raw depths, of the tomb, of flowers. I smelled its smell and started crying, unafraid. . . . I wept so bitterly, fully, happily, as I have never wept again in all my life.

Before the fact of irrational violence the father's bourgeois ac-
counting—whereby reward should equal effort—proves futile. The
boy of these stories is an exploited child living out his father's
dreams. When those dreams collapse, when life proves to be un-
predictable and uncontrollable, the child slips into the formlessness
of hysteria, which he experiences as a kind of release. In his desperate
need he seeks out his mother, and also other men.

His choice lands on opposites of his father, men who live, not
in an abstract future, but in the concrete present. Some of his
substitute fathers are Gentile, others Jewish: their common trait is
physical presence. In a world threatening to dissolve into nightmare,
the drowning boy reaches out to them as to anchors of reality.
During the panic of his examination, as "a feeling of complete
oblivion" comes over him, his eye lights on the compassionate
Pyatnitsky. The physicality of the kindly old man sticks in the boy's
mind: "he halted for a moment, the frock coat flowing down his
back in a slow heavy wave. I discerned embarrassment in the large,
fleshy, upper-class back, and got closer to the old man. 'Children,'
he said to the boys, 'don't touch this lad.' And he laid a fat hand
tenderly on my shoulder." He loves his granduncle Shoyl: "I loved
that boastful old man, for he sold fish at the market. His fat hands
were moist, covered with fish-scales, and smelled of worlds chill
and beautiful." Shoyl not only touches life in his work, but he is
also an artist of sorts. He makes things (the boy's dovecot) and he
tells yarns that the adult narrator recognizes as the lies of an ignorant
man, but it does not matter, for "they were good stories." Shoyl is
also a fighter who resists his anti-Semitic murderers. Kuzma, the
third of the men the boy turns to when his father fails him, recites
Shoyl's eulogy: "He cursed them all good and proper, cursed them
to the bone, it was just grand."

It would be wrong to say that Babel rejected his Jewish past.
Rather he rejects Jewish passivity and subservience. Jews hoping to
escape their tragic circumstances by winning prestige and the approval of others strike him as sterile. They are pursuing a will-o'-
the-wisp, the empty form of achievement without its substance.
Men rooted in nature, in physical reality, whether Gentile or Jewish,
win Babel's sympathy; he is on the side of those who act and create.
Creation, he told Paustovsky, is a kind of action; it is not only a
making of things but a way of being in the world. Through art a
man may achieve what really counts—integrity and self-definition. [1]

In his rebellion against middle-class pieties and his assertion of the individualism of the artist Babel was acting very much in the spirit of Russian modernism. No doubt it was his instinctive hostility toward bourgeois values rather than ideological faith that led him to accept the Russian Revolution.

Style

In the *Dovecot* cycle Babel moves away from the fanciful whimsicality of the *Odessa Tales* and the rhapsodic lyricism of *Red Cavalry*. The narration is fuller, more detailed and "realistic," closer to the traditional norms of the short story. Character and incident, instead of being submerged in a decorative pattern, stand out in relief. The biographical subject matter finds a corresponding sequential form, a "before" followed by a "then." Shifts in the narrative plane are not so abrupt as in the earlier fiction. The stories are told in the relaxed manner of the raconteur rather than the tensely concentrated style of the poet: "When I was a child I longed for a dovecot. Never in all my life have I wanted a thing more. I was nine years old when my father promised the money to buy the wood and three pairs of pigeons. It was 1904, I was studying for the entrance exam to the preparatory class of the secondary school at Nikolaev" . . . (*I*, 209).

Nevertheless, it is not an entirely new Babel that we encounter in the *Dovecot* cycle. In turning to a historical narration in which the tale to be told is in the forefront, he curbs but does not completely eliminate familiar expressive means. Repetitions and syntactical parallelisms (also a kind of repetition) are among his favorite devices. Through repetition language turns in upon itself, achieving a compactness more characteristic of lyric poetry than narrative prose. A repeated phrase tends to lyrical or rhetorical expansiveness, though any literary manner, when exaggerated or employed in an incongruous context, may result in parody.

Though lyricism was present in the *Odessa Tales*—"Dusk had settled across the yard, dusk flowed like an evening wave on a wide river . . ."—the overall tone was comic. Here repetition was employed to achieve a mock-heroic tone, as hyperbolic rhetoric coated a homely content: "But does the foamy surge of the Odessa sea cast roast chicken on the shore? . . . fat-bellied jars of Jamaican rum, oily Madeira, cigars from the plantations of Pierpont Morgan, and oranges from the environs of Jerusalem. That is what [*vot chto*] the

foaming surge of the Odessa sea casts upon the shore, that is what
[*vot chto*] comes the way of Odessa beggars at Jewish weddings.
Jamaica rum came their way at the wedding of Dvoyra Krik."
Repetition may also create the feel of oral narration. In writing we
try to develop our thoughts logically and sequentially; in speaking
we tend to repeat ourselves: "Are words necessary? A man was and
is no more. A harmless bachelor was living his life like a bird on
a bough. . . . There came a Jew . . . and took a potshot. . . .
Are words necessary?" (*I*, 186, 162, 169).

In *Red Cavalry* repetitions contribute to the work's poetic atmosphere. They shape hypnotic incantations, evoking the mysteries
of Catholic Poland or Jewish Hasidism: "I can see you now, faithless
monk, in your mauve cossack, with your plump hands and your
soul as gentle and pitiless as the soul of a cat; I can see the wounds
of your god oozing seed, a fragrant poison to intoxicate virgins."
"Here before me is the market, and the death of the market."
Syntactical parallelism is at the heart of Babel's liturgical manner,
his "Hebraic" style: "Oh the rotted Talmuds of my childhood. Oh
the dense melancholy of memories!" "Oh death, Oh covetous one,
Oh greedy thief, why couldst thou not have spared us, just for
once?" He strengthens the effect by the use of exclamations and
interrogatives, and also by placing the prose into direct speech. In
"The Rabbi's Son" Babel introduces a character whose only function
is to hear the narrator's address: "Do you remember Zhitomir,
Vasily? Do you remember the river Teterev, Vasily, and that night
when the Sabbath, the young Sabbath, crept along the sunset,
crushing the stars beneath her little red heel?" Refrains frame a
passage, turning it into an enclosed artistic miniature: "There are
no bees left in Volhynia. We defiled the hives. We destroyed them
with sulphur and blew them up with gunpowder. The smell of
singed rags reeked in the sacred republic of the bees. Dying, they
flew around slowly, humming so that you could hardly hear. And
we who had no bread extracted the honey with our swords. There
were no bees left in Volhynia" (*I*, 30, 50, 81, 149, 60).[2]

Though such refrains still form part of the fabric of the *Dovecot*
cycle, separating passages into small islands in the general flow of
language, they no longer transmit the parodic playfulness of the
Odessa Tales or the magical strangeness of *Red Cavalry*. Repetition
sometimes merely highlights a passage: "I had a knack for book
learning. The teachers, though they employed cunning, could not

rob me of my intelligence and avid memory. I had a knack for book learning and got top marks in both subjects [Russian and arithmetic]." Only occasionally does a repetition shape the sort of decorative passage that is both a strength and weakness of Babel's prose, embroidering it with much beauty but at times weighting it excessively. The colorful epithets, striking metaphors, unusual turns of speech are still there—"crimson blindness," "his coarse face made of red fat, fists, and iron," "her hip moved and breathed," "the world's blueness," "night stood erect in the poplars, stars lay on the bent boughs," "the smoke of the universe," "the sounds dripped from my fiddle like iron filings"—but they are less frequent (*I*, 209–10, 216, 221, 224, 249, 252, 257). After *Red Cavalry* Babel started to make himself over into a less exotic kind of writer.

The Story as Symbol

Metaphors decrease in number in these later stories. Lyricism is muted, the language is that of the storyteller rather than the poet. However, Babel's fiction not only uses metaphors; it *is* metaphoric. His stories, though rooted in actuality, transcend the particulars of experience to reach universals of existence. Thus in *Red Cavalry* the conflict of Cossack and Jew is simultaneously a confrontation of history and culture, action and compassion, a masculine and a feminine principle. At the moment of the boy's crisis "The Story of My Dovecot" breaks away from its mimetic form to become something much more moving and with broader implications than a factual reminiscence of childhood. His trauma is an event of intense poetic concentration, an epiphany in which the boy's consciousness leaps to a vision of the nature of things. Here Babel shows himself the kind of writer he is. His renderings of the texture of everyday life—what Russians call *byt*—usually do not stand as ends in themselves, but are subordinate to his imaginative preoccupations. Babel is possessed by certain images or metaphors, and thus his work, even when the surface is apparently realistic, reaches to symbolic form. Hence, the tendency of each individual work to collapse into a fragment or, as he put it, a "chapter" of a larger design. As the boy hears Woe ride across the trampled earth on a great steed, as he presses against the damp earth smelling of raw depths, of the tomb, and of flowers, we are at once transported into the pages of *Red Cavalry*. The boundaries separating individual works are shadowy and easily breached by a central metaphor of life. Once again a Babelian protagonist confronts a universe of violence which makes the values and ways of the culture that had previously sustained him seem futile. The props removed from under him, he teeters at the edge of an abyss of meaninglessness and again seeks comfort in the womb of the maternal earth, an escape that the whisperings of his mind tell him is really a tomb of the spirit.

"First Love"

"The Story of My Dovecot" is a masterpiece. Urbane and deliciously ironic, it nevertheless penetrates to tragic pain. In the other stories of the cycle misfortune is still part of the scene of childhood, but the tone is lighter. The author looks back upon the disasters of his youth with the wisdom won by experience. The wry irony of maturity keeps the anguish at bay: "I saw those kisses from my window. They caused me agony, but what's the use of talking about it? The love and the jealousy of a ten-year-old boy are in every way the same as the love and jealousy of a grown-up" (I, 221).

"First Love" picks up where "The Story of My Dovecot" ends. Kuzma, the janitor, rushes the boy off to Gentile neighbors, the Rubtsovs, where he will be safe from the pogrom. The Rubtsovs enjoy a flagrant sensuality alien to puritanical Jewish culture. Galina Rubtsov's opulence is the stuff of which adolescent daydreams are made. As in the *Odessa Tales*, the irony is in the excess. Thus Galina, we are told,

would glide through the rooms with her braid hanging down her back, wearing elegant red shoes and a Chinese robe. Under the lace of her low-cut slip one could see her breasts, white, bulging, pressed downward, and the depths between them. On her robe were embroidered pink silk dragons, birds, trees with hollows.

All day long she ambled about with a vague smile on her moist lips, brushing against unpacked trunks and ladders for gymnastics strewn about the floor. Galina would bruise herself, pull the robe above her knees, and say to her husband, "Kiss the boo-boo."

The boy is ecstatic over such uninhibited displays of self-indulgence, but also fearful: "her gaze frightened me, I would turn away and tremble. I saw in her eyes an amazing and shameful side of human life, and I longed to fall into an uncommon sleep, to forget about that life surpassing all my dreams."

The title "First Love" would immediately recall to Russian readers a classic story of 1859 of the same name by Ivan Turgenev about loss of innocence. In Babel's version Galina incites imaginings of the mysteries of sex, and a chance incident furthers his education in violence and power. Through the window of the Rubtsovs' house he witnesses his father's humiliation. His father, helpless before rioters looting his store, appeals to a passing Cossack officer.

I saw through the window the empty street under the vast sky, and my redheaded father walking along in the roadway. He walked bareheaded, his soft red hair fluttering, his paper dickey askew and fastened to the wrong button. . . .

The officer rode slowly, not looking right or left. He rode as though through a mountain pass, where one can only look ahead.

"Captain," my father mumbled . . . , "captain," my father said, grasping his head in his hands and kneeling in the mud.

"Do what I can," the officer answered, still looking straight ahead, and raising his hand in its lemon-colored chamois glove to the peak of his cap. . . .

"Look," my father said, still on his knees, "they are smashing everything dear to me. Captain, why is it?"

The officer murmured something, and again put the lemon glove to his cap. He touched the reins but his horse did not move. My father crawled in front of the horse on his knees, rubbing up against its short, kindly, tousled legs.

"At your service," the officer said, tugged at the reins, and rode off, the Cossacks following. They sat passionless on their tall saddles, riding through an imaginary mountain pass and disappearing into Cathedral Street.

The boy has moved into the "vast skies" of *Red Cavalry*. The Cossack could very well have ridden into "First Love" from its pages, and his father might be one of its hapless victims. As in "The Story of My Dovecot," the tale suddenly opens to a symbolic vision of another order of existence lying beyond the ordinary hopes and dreams of middle-class Jews. Again crisis explodes into a common comedy of the confusions of growing up, giving the story an imaginative scope and intensity it would otherwise lack. Under a vast sky, eyes fixed on some mysterious mountain pass, men ride on great stallions, heedless of the boy's plight. The impersonality of history intrudes into his tiny world of examinations and prized pigeons. (Among the items the looters have hurled out of the store is a photograph of the boy in his recently won school uniform.) Events stubbornly refuse to conform to private desires. His father's humiliation is profoundly wounding, as it would be for any boy his age. Perhaps even more traumatic is the revelation of the impotence of the values he has been taught. In the face of brute power, lives predicated on a symmetry of effort and gain, virtue and reward, lose their meaning. Again, it is his mother who makes sense. "Lousy money," she says to her husband, "you gave up everything for it. A human life, the children, our wretched scrap of happiness. . . ."

The boy suffers another bout of hysteria, with an uncontrollable fit of hiccoughing which Galina vainly tries to remedy. Looking at her, he imagines that he is a member of the Jewish Defense Corps of Odessa, organized to resist anti-Semitic rioters: "On my shoulder a worthless rifle hangs by a green cord. I am kneeling by a wooden fence shooting at the murderers. . . . The antiquated rifle shoots badly. The murderers have beards and white teeth, they approach stealthily. I have a proud feeling of imminent death, and in the sky, in the world's blueness, I see Galina. . . . she smiles mockingly. Her husband, the officer, half-dressed, stands behind her, kissing her neck."

The daydream expresses an adolescent wish for power and revenge, and Oedipal anxiety over failure and retribution. After the painful scene of his father's degradation the narrator has resumed his posture of ironic distance. Behind the suffering child we are aware of the adult author looking back understandingly upon the confusions of childhood. However, such confusions have a way of determining the course of a life, or the shape of art in the case of an artist. Whether the event described happened at all, whether it happened as it is described, is moot and perhaps trivial. What is clear enough is that Babel carried away from his childhood a repulsion against submissiveness and a fascination with heroism. How to reconcile the appeal of heroic action with compassion for suffering became his problem.

"In the Basement"

"In the Basement" is less imaginative than the other stories of the cycle. Unenriched by poetic leaps, it is a comedy of manners, of domestic disorder. The family of the *Dovecot* stories has its share of crazy relatives. The end of "First Love" saw the hiccoughing youth packed off to live with Grandfather Leivi-Itzkhok and Uncle Simon in Odessa. Here he also discovers an Aunt Bobka, who, like his mother, is the only sensible person in a household of unstable men. Grandfather Leivi-Itzkhok, a former rabbi thrown out of his village for forging a Polish count's signature on a bill of exchange, spends his time writing a book in Hebrew entitled "The Headless Man." Uncle Simon is a loud and argumentative drunk.

The boy, bookish and lonely, makes a friend from the upper crust of Odessa's Jewish community, Mark Borgman. Mark's father, the manager of the Russian Bank for Foreign Trade, has risen so high in the world that he refuses to speak even Russian, much less Yiddish, preferring the coarse English he has picked up from Liverpool ship captains. Mark is a top student, unlike our daydreaming hero who does less well. Mark invites him to the family villa.

Just as hyperbole characterizes Babel's heroic (and mock-heroic) style, it also marks his satiric moments. Everything in the home of these Jewish parvenus is excessive, especially their women: "Card addicts and sweet-tooths, slovenly female fops with secret vices, scented lingerie, and enormous thighs, the women snapped their black fans and staked gold coins. Through the fence of wild vine the sun reached at them, its fiery disc enormous. Bronzed gleams lent weight to the women's black hair. Drops of sunset sparkled in their diamonds—diamonds disposed in every possible place: in the depths of splayed bosoms, in painted ears, on puffy bluish she-animal fingers."

The impressionable child is flabbergasted by the wealth of the Borgmans and their easy confidence in the opportunities life offers them. Insecure and unhappy, he allows his fancy to run wild: driven by shame over the poverty of his home and his disreputable relatives, he concocts outlandish tales about their adventures. When Mark returns his visit, he stows his eccentric grandfather with a neighbor and packs the boisterous uncle off to a tavern.

But they of course return unexpectedly, and the boy's plans dissolve into comic chaos. In a highly theatrical scene Uncle Simon, a compulsive collector of odd pieces of furniture, enters drunk and staggering under the weight of a bizarre clothes rack made of antlers as well as a red trunk with fittings shaped like lions' jaws. Grandfather, not to be outdone, joins the party, scraping away on his

fiddle. Thinking that his stratagem was working, the boy had begun
to recite Marc Antony's speech "Friends, Romans, countrymen,"
and now keeps right on, desperately hoping to drown out his uncle's
obscenities, but only adding a counterpoint to the hubbub. Mark
slips away in embarrassment. The conclusion of the story reminds
us that experience which is entertaining from a distance may be
very painful close up: the humiliated child makes a clumsy attempt
at drowning himself in a water barrel. Getting no sympathy from
his crazy grandfather, he breaks into tears, the only release for this
lonely victim of a disordered family: "And the world of tears was
so enormous, so beautiful that everything, save tears, fled from my
eyes."

"Awakening"

"Awakening" is one of Babel's most lovely stories. Its theme is
still the hurt of childhood, its fears and loneliness, but here the
child moves from confusion to understanding and self-assertion in
a tale of discovery, of "awakening." Choices are made, a path decided
upon, so that pain can be put to the side and life go on. Like *Red
Cavalry*, the *Dovecot* quartet ends in acceptance. However, where
Red Cavalry concludes with a stoical affirmation of the will to live
despite the world's cruelty, "Awakening" is more hopeful. It puts
a final seal upon the story of a childhood that, for all its heartbreak,
is essentially comic. Woe rides on great steeds across the screen of
the child's imagination in prophecy of things to come, of terrible
dangers that threaten his world and ours, but for the moment life,
though confusing and messy, is not tragically impossible.

In "Awakening" the models of manhood among which the child
must pick are perhaps more easily grasped than in the other stories
of the cycle. Instead of the schematic division between Jew and
Gentile that much commentary on Babel has emphasized, three
paths present themselves to the child: his father's, Grandfather Leivi-
Itzkhok's, and that of two Gentiles who teach him things he never
learned at home.

"Though my father could have reconciled himself to poverty, he
had to have fame"—once again, the son is prepared for sacrifice on
the altar of his father's ambitions. "Our fathers had thought up a
lottery, building it on the bones of little children." Too often these
young Davids of the mind, groomed to vindicate the Jewish people

and preserve it from menacing Goliaths, turn out to be stunted children, crippled by the enormous burdens loaded on their frail shoulders. In "Awakening" his father selects music as the arena where the boy will distinguish himself, not because he has shown even a shred of musical talent, but because Odessa had nurtured a series of child prodigies: Mischa Elman, Efrem Zimbalist, Jascha Heifetz. The manager of this "lottery" in which many take their chances but few are chosen is Mr. Zagursky, a music teacher with "a factory of infant prodigies." The description of the school is a piece of ironic grotesquerie that pointedly isolates the scene from ordinary, healthy life: the study is a "sanctum"; those who enter it "dwarfs," "hysterics," initiates of a "sect."

The child of these stories is the victim of two kinds of violence: that of anti-Semitic rioters and that of Jewish fathers who try to twist their children into becoming something they are not. The first he can do little about; against the second he rebels. But even as he spurns the compensatory psychology of men hoping to overcome their failure through the triumphs of their children, he heeds other Jewish voices, forebears in whom he perceives inspiration of another sort. He turns to eccentric misfits who have ignored the bourgeois ladder of success. Like Gedali of *Red Cavalry,* his crazy relatives march to their own drumbeat. Quasi-artists, bohemians of the ghetto, they have refused to dwell in airy dreams of future glory. Instead they make things and know things. Uncle Shoyl knows about fish and can build a dovecot; Grandfather Leivi-Itzkhok is a mine of information: "My grandfather . . . was the laughingstock of the town, and its chief adornment. He used to walk about the streets in a top hat and old boots, dissipating doubt in the darkest of cases. He would be asked what a Gobelin was, why the Jacobins betrayed Robespierre, how you make artificial silk, what a Caesarian section was. And my grandfather could answer these questions. . . . Grandfather Leivi-Itzkhok, who went cracked as he grew old, spent his whole life writing a tale entitled 'The Headless Man.' I took after him."

The *Dovecot* cycle may be read as a boy's search for a father to assume the role of his own failed father, and also a search for a model of the artist. Art was a way of escaping the inhibitions and hypocrisies of bourgeois life, a route by which one might discover his true self. From his nonconformist relatives the boy inherits the Jewish passion for learning, not as an instrument of gain but for

its own sake, and the Jewish gift of talk, its love of the colorful
yarn. Like Grandfather Leivi-Itzkhok, author of the never-to-be-
completed epos of "The Headless Man," he stores up odd bits of
information colored by his overheated imagination; like Uncle Shoyl,
"a simple-minded liar" whose tall tales he has never forgotten, for
"they were good stories," he is "an untruthful little boy. . . . my
imagination was always working overtime" (I, 213, 247).
    But these fabulists of the ghetto are too bizarre for the boy to
follow unreservedly. Alienated by secularization from the sustaining
order of a religious tradition, isolated by prejudice from the dominant culture, they have become cranks. These are the charming
but eccentric Odessa street-corner philosophers whose fate Babel
swore to Paustovsky at all costs to avoid. The child takes from
Jewish life its emotional richness but flees its accompanying hysteria.
In the harbor, among friendly Gentiles, he discovers the possibility
of liberation, and also a notion of how creative expressiveness can
be disciplined.
    Discrimination had restricted Jewish entry into the crafts or ag-
riculture, relegating many to the position of middle men—salesmen, pedlars, storekeepers, tax collectors—dealing in the abstract
relations of money exchange. Mr. Trottyburn, an old sailor who
smuggles his brother's carved pipes into Odessa, introduces the boy
into the mysterious delights of craftsmanship. Trottyburn speaks in
impassioned defense of hand-made artifacts: "Gentlemen, . . . take
my word, the pets must be made with your own hands. . . ."
Imagination, as Babel showed in his early satiric sketch "Inspiration," is cheap if not anchored in the disciplines of craftsmanship.
However, craft is not a mechanical exercise; it is an expression of
love. The craftsman has a profoundly personal relation to his object.
His loving care turns inert material into living things—not mere
pipes but "pets," each of them an organic whole, particular and yet
universal: "The pipes of the Lincolnshire master breathed poetry.
In each one of them thought was invested, a drop of eternity." Like
Uncle Shoyl and Grandfather Leivi-Itzkhok, the Lincolnshire master
(Trottyburn's brother) is a man "who refused to swim with the
tide." Unlike them, however, he has the good fortune to have located
an ordering principle in his life.
    In his fine book The World of Sholom Aleichem, Maurice Samuel
notes the poverty of Yiddish vocabulary for flowers, trees, animals,
and birds.[3] Crowded into urban ghettoes and villages, Jews lived

lives remote from nature. As Trottyburn shows him the joys of craftsmanship, a second Gentile, the kindly Efim Nikitich, initiates him into the joys of nature. Nikitich takes pity on repressed and frightened Jewish boys; he teaches them songs, gymnastics, swimming. The young boy's writings interest him, though he laments the absence of any feel for nature in them.

Nikitich encourages an attitude to nature that is not one of passive appreciation. It is, like Trottyburn's teaching, a lesson in power. For the boy's father and his friends power is an abstract dream to be realized in an unreal future, the glory and wealth to be won by their children. For Trottyburn and Nikitich, on the other hand, the possibility of power is here and now: the craftsman's power to shape and create, and every man's power to act. Swimming is, like art, a discipline. The artist brings formless matter under his control; the swimmer orders the movements of his body to master the element in which he moves. Under Nikitich's tutelage the boy learns to wed knowledge to action: "How slow was my acquisition of the things one needs to know. In my childhood, chained to the Gemara [the second part of the Talmud], I had led the life of a sage. When I grew up I started climbing trees." Nikitich's instruction in "natural philosophy" is again a lesson in mastery. Like Adam, he names things in order to gain power over them:

He pointed with his stick at a tree with a reddish trunk and a low crown.
"What's that tree?"
I didn't know.
"What's growing on that bush?"
I didn't know this either. . . .
"What bird is that singing?"
I knew none of the answers. The names of trees and birds, their division into species, where birds fly away to, on which side the sun rises, when the dew falls thickest—all these things were unknown to me.
"And you dare to write! A man who doesn't live in nature, as a stone does or an animal, will never in all his life write two worthwhile lines. Your landscapes are like stage props. In heaven's name, what have your parents been thinking of for fourteen years?"
What *had* they been thinking of? Of protested bills of exchange, of Mischa Elman's mansions.

Each of the four *Dovecot* stories ends in flight. In the first two, however, the boy is passively packed off to another place—in the

title story to the Rubtsovs' to save him from the pogrom, in "First
Love" to Odessa to cure him from his nervous ailment. In "In the
Basement" the choice is his own, but it is taken in despair. He has
grown to a point where he recognizes the moral confusions and
hollow ambitions of his family, but the self-complacent nouveau-
riche Borgmans do not represent a believable alternative. Feeling
trapped, he attempts suicide. In "Awakening" the doors open to
the possibilities of a life of creativity. Through literature men overcome the helplessness of formless existence by naming things and
making things. At the end of the story the boy's truancy from
Zagursky's musical torture chamber is discovered and the tale explodes into a whirlwind of comic hysteria: execrations, threats, wails
of self-pity. The boy's first impulse is once again to flee inward.
He locks himself in that last refuge of a harried childhood—the
bathroom. But by now he is old enough to imagine the possibility
of the only true escape, building a life of one's own:

I sat it out in my fortress till nightfall. When all had gone to bed, Aunt
Bobka took me to grandmother's. We had a long way to go. The moonlight
froze on bushes unknown to me, on trees that had no name. Some anon-
ymous bird emitted a whistle and faded away, perhaps in sleep. What
bird was it? What was it called? Does dew fall in the evening? Where is
the constellation of the Great Bear? On what side does the sun rise?
    We were going along Post Office Street. Aunt Bobka held me firmly
by the hand so that I shouldn't run away. She was right to. I was thinking
of running away.

Chapter Eight
Plays and Films

Theater of the early twentieth century underwent the same revolt against realism and naturalism that reshaped prose fiction. Symbolist drama broke the hold of realistic illusionism. The play was now viewed, not as a *trompe d'oeil* designed to give the appearance of reality, but as an invention of art. For the symbolist playwright day-to-day life was a mere husk hiding the kernel of truth. Seeking the essence of things rather than their mode of existence, he hoped, through suggestion, allusion, symbol, and myth to reach beyond the silence of concrete objects to eternal verities of the soul. The symbolists cultivated a play of lyrical moods and allegorical meanings. More interested in universal truth than individual psychology, they muted the conflicts of motive which are the stuff of drama. Though their experiments left a mark on the modern theater, the lyrical and literary character of symbolist drama—its use of the hieratic language of a mystical coterie—made it a genre enjoyed more readily in the privacy of the study than in the public arena of the theater.

Around 1910—the high-water mark of Russian symbolism—the inevitable reaction set in. Playwrights and directors—most notably the brilliant Vsevolod Meyerhold—wanted plays that could be performed and not merely read. The innovators, however, did not revert to the habits of naturalistic drama. Instead they emphasized theatricality, the play as spectacle. As in the case of prose fiction and poetry, the avant-garde, while rebelling against the symbolist credo, continued, sometimes unwittingly, to adhere to some of its principles. Like their symbolist mentors, the post-1910 generation insisted that the work was a creation of the artistic imagination (in the theater, the director's as well as the author's), not an image dictated by external reality like a face in a mirror or a figure on photographic paper. The play was *play*. Audiences should not be duped into thinking that what they were witnessing was "real life," but were to be made fully conscious of the artificiality of art. They were to be aware they were at a performance. Symbolism had dreamed of destroying realistic illusionism in order to create a theater of ritual where actors and audience might join in a communal reenactment of eternal mysteries of the spirit. The post-1910 generation undertook an analogous job of demolition, but with differing purposes. The play could still speak to our need for truth, but it should also be fun—like the circus, where we know very well that everything is artifice, but that only adds to our entertainment.

Sunset

Babel worked on the play *Zakat* (Sunset) in 1926 and 1927.[1] First produced in 1928 by the Moscow Art Theater, it ran for only sixteen performances. Like much Soviet writing of the twenties, the play is a hybrid. Symbolism was more than a literary manner. In Russia it marked a last desperate attempt of the non-Marxist intelligentsia to forge a coherent culture in face of the fragmentation of modern life. Upon its collapse, artists seeking to create new forms chose their models where they might. The disintegration of a dominant artistic trend, even one as short-lived as symbolism, is usually followed by a period of eclecticism. As the writers of the twenties turned to the contemporary world about them, to a new realism, residues of the symbolist style filtered into their work. In *Red Cavalry* a stark naturalism coexists with metaphorical allusiveness and lyricism. Similarly, in *Sunset* a naturalist surface is molded into a symbolic design. Though reminiscent of Gorky's family dramas, *Sunset* is yet too playfully humorous to be confused with the melodramas of that humorless writer. Its symbolism and theatricality at times recall the modernist plays of Leonid Andreev, though without their allegorical abstractions and metaphysical pretensions.

A reworking of the *Odessa Tales, Sunset* takes its cue from an incidental sentence in one of them: "Mendel Krik sat at one of the tables drinking wine from a green tumbler and relating how he had been crippled by his own sons—the elder Benya and the younger Lyovka."[2] The center of gravity has shifted from Benya the son to Mendel the father, a strong-willed man who runs a large carting business in Odessa. Impetuous as his son Benya, at the age when men hear time's winged chariot drawing near, he plans to run away with a young woman. His sons fear that their father will squander their inheritance on his infatuation. They get into a brawl, Benya strikes his father with the butt of his revolver, locks him up in his house, and takes over the business. The father declines into the sad impotence of useless old age. The sons, especially flamboyant Benya, assume power. Mendel's sunset is their sunrise.

This plot of generational conflict, though it holds the eight scenes of the play together, is submerged in a good deal of ethnographic material. As in the *Odessa Tales,* Babel is interested at least as much in portraying the society of the Jewish ghetto of Moldavanka as in telling a story. Incidental situations—for example, sister Dvoyra's courtship by the storekeeper Boyarsky—and comic interludes, such as the hilarious synagogue service of scene 5, are freely interspersed with the action. A host of characters are paraded before our eyes only because they are charming. Language becomes part of the scenery, a sign of the milieu. In traditional drama speech was to a large extent determined by the demands of the plot. In *Sunset,* as in Chekhov's groundbreaking plays and the modern drama that grows out of them, people often talk about anything but the issue at hand—their business affairs, local gossip, the meaning of life.

A milieu comes to life at the price of one-dimensionality of character, in which *Sunset* also resembles the *Odessa Tales.* In the stories Benya was a cartoon, but a richly colored one; in the plays he has turned flat. Much of his flashy insouciance is gone, and a streak of meanness surfaces in him. Though not a psychological writer, in his fiction Babel employed the narrator's reflections to place his accurately perceived but intellectually limited characters into wider contexts of irony and meaning. They may be all surface, but their creator is interesting. In a play, however, characters must speak for themselves, and Benya, Lyovka, and Mendel do not have much to say. Though the play has considerable vitality, its appeal lies not in the dramatic confrontation of the major characters but in the gallery of quaint Moldavankans who troop across the stage.

Sunset is a "slice of life" but a life that is slightly wacky. The language displays a comic formalism that puts the characters, if not in the never-never land of fantasy, then in a place quite removed from the world as we know it or expect it to be. The Moldavankans lard their conversation with aphorisms, proverbs, citations from commentaries to the Torah; they habitually repeat themselves (repetitions serve as comic signatures of a character), use odd expressions, and shape their speech into rhythmic phrases. As in the *Odessa Tales,* homely everyday life becomes picturesque through the quirkiness of language.

BENYA: (*knotting his tie*) Pop, if you catch my drift, can't stand parting with the dowry.

LYOVKA: Slit the old man's throat, along with all pigs!

ARYE-LEIB: Is that a way to talk about a father, Lyovka?

LYOVKA: Let him not be a bum.

ARYE-LEIB: Your father is older than you by a Saturday.

LYOVKA: Let him not be a lout.

BENYA: (*sticking a pearl pin into his tie*) Last year Semka Munsh wanted Dvoyra, but Pop, if you catch my drift, can't stand parting with the dowry. He made mincemeat with sauce out of Semka's kisser and threw him down the stairs, one step at a time.

LYOVKA: Slit the old man's throat, along with all pigs!

ARYE-LEIB: About a matchmaker like me it has been said by Ibn-Ezra: "If you propose, o mortal, to become a candle-maker, then the sun will stand still in mid-heaven like a curbstone and never set."

LYOVKA: (*to his mother*) A hundred times a day the old man murders us, and you're as silent as a fence-post. Any minute her boy friend might hop in. . . .

ARYE-LEIB: It has been said about me by Ibn-Ezra: "If you propose to sew shrouds for corpses, not one man will die from here to eternity. Amen!"

BENYA: (*knots his tie, throws off a crimson band supporting his hair-do, wraps himself in a dock-tailed coat, and pours himself a tumbler of vodka*) Health to all present!

LYOVKA: . . . Good health.

ARYE-LEIB: May all go well.

MONSIEUR BOYARSKY: (*a lively, roly-poly man, dashes into the room. He runs off at the mouth without stop*) Greetings! Greetings! . . . Very pleased, extraordinarily pleased! Greetings!

ARYE-LEIB: You promised to be here at four, Lazar, and it's already six.

BOYARSKY: . . . My God, we live in Odessa, and in our Odessa there are customers who pluck the life out of you as you pluck the pit from a date. There are good friends ready to eat you in your clothes and without salt. There are car-loads of troubles, scandals by the thousands. How can a man think about his health, and anyhow what can a storekeeper do with health? It took all I had to run over to the sea baths—and then straight to you.

ARYE-LEIB: So you take sea baths, Lazar?

BOYARSKY: Every other day, like clockwork.

ARYE-LEIB: (*to the old woman*) You can't get away with less than fifty kopecks for a sea bath.

BOYARSKY: My God, wine flows in our Odessa. The Greek market, Fanconi's. . . .

ARYE-LEIB: You eat at Fanconi's, Lazar?

BOYARSKY: I eat at Fanconi's.

ARYE-LEIB: (*in triumph*) He eats at Fanconi's. (*I*, 324–26)

The most ordinary conversations are cast in the rhythmical chantings of liturgy. Arye-Leib instructing a boy in the Torah sounds much the same as Mendel and a customer chatting about business. As in symbolist drama (and the plays of Chekhov), separate conversations are counterpointed in a way more musical than dramatic.

ARYE-LEIB: "By night on my bed I sought. Whom did I seek?" Rashi teaches us.

BOY: Rashi teaches us—"sought the Torah" . . .

BENYA: Time passes. Out of its way, Lyovka. Make way for time! . . .

BOBRINETS: (*in a deafening voice*) Mendel, if you won't carry my wheat to the harbor, who will carry it? If I cannot turn to you, to whom can I turn?

MENDEL: There are other people in the world besides Mendel. There are other carting businesses besides my carting business.

BOBRINETS: In Odessa there is no carting business besides yours. . . . (*I*, 345–46)

The language of pathos is as stylized as the language of comedy. When the ferocious Mendel is subdued by his sons, like a King Lear of the ghetto, he bursts into rhetorical grandiloquence. His declamation mounts to pathetic heights through a series of syntactical parallelisms and rhythmic phrases, rounded off by emphatic interrogatives and imperatives: "Why won't you unlock the gates, Nikifor? Why won't you let me out of the yard where I've spent my life? . . . This yard saw me as father of my children, husband of my wife, master of my horses. It saw my power, and my twenty stallions, and twelve wagons fastened by iron. It saw my legs, huge as posts, and my hands, these cruel hands of mine. And now, my dear sons, unlock the gates for me. Let today be as I wish it. Let me depart from this yard which has seen too much" (*I*, 352).

Comic play and rhetorical embroidery work against the naturalistic elements in the play, as does its symbolic structure. Mendel and his sons, uninteresting in themselves, are actors in an ageless plot that points to a final moral. The universal drama of rise and fall, of sunrise and sunset, is the play's true action, to which the motivation and behavior of the characters are subordinate. Had Mendel and his sons behaved differently, the former would still have fallen, and the latter, barring accident, have risen, as inevitably as sunset follows sunrise. The stage directions indicate the play's symbolic character as they describe a movement from light to dark, from day through sunset to black night. Scene 3, set in a Russian tavern, is especially close to symbolist drama and the experimental theater it spawned. The stage is dark, Mendel calls desperately for light, a chorus of blind men and women enter singing of the sea, a second chorus of drunkards comment on the strange goings-on. Their speeches, like much of the dialogue of the play, are saturated with symbolic implication—they ask whether Mendel would turn night into day. (As the aging Mendel belongs to night and darkness, so the young Benya is, as his mother calls him, the "sun" [*I*, 330].) The synagogue scene (5), though comic, falls into a similar musical pattern as solemn Hebrew prayers are humorously contrasted with the business talk of the Moldavankan wheelers and dealers, while Benya surreptitiously plans a robbery.

Though the play makes use of symbolist techniques, it never lapses into the schematism of allegory. Its rough-hewn characters, with their raw, vigorous speech, have too much life in them to evaporate into abstract formulas. The post-1910 generation reacted against the ethereal manner of much symbolist writing, and *Sunset* may be viewed as an attempt to give backbone to its airy forms, to bring them down to earth.

Among the symbolic resonances of the play are echoes of the Garden of Eden. Mendel defies time. He wants to cling to the noontime of his life forever, to escape its inevitable sunset. Dreaming of running off to Bessarabia with his ravishing Russian nymphette, whose scheming mother has tempted him with visions of carefree apple orchards, he cries out, "There is no end, no limit. . . . I'm smarter than God" (*I, 333*). Voices in the tavern ask whether he is trying to turn night into day, Monday into Sunday. Mendel seeks an eternal Sabbath of joy, paradise in the gardens of youth. Benya appreciates that ambition. "I want the Sabbath to be the Sabbath," he exclaims at the end of the play. Let us enjoy the holiday season of our lives while we have it, he says. Let us live fully, in joy, not mixing water with the wine in our glasses or in our hearts. Cut from the same cloth as his father, he understands and forgives him.

Sunset moves in a circle from the abortive celebration of scene 1, broken up by family squabbles, to the fulfilled celebration of scene 8, in which father and sons are reconciled and the long-suffering virgin Dvoyra is, it seems, finally to marry. Since a play normally lacks a narrator to meditate upon the proceedings, Babel employs two characters to perform that function: Arye-Leib and Rabbi ben Zkharya. The latter comes on stage at the end to sum up. In tragedy the hero is destroyed for refusing to accept or failing to recognize the order of the universe. In comedy men and women, unless they are unmitigated scoundrels, learn to accept the way of the world, and even, as in *Sunset,* to celebrate it. Ben Zkharya proclaims the wisdom of acceptance. Joshua, the son of Nun, who stopped the sun in heaven, was a wicked madman. "And now," he says, we see that Mendel Krik, a member of our synagogue, has turned out to be no "wiser than Joshua, the son of Nun. He wanted to warm himself in the sun all his life long, he wanted to remain all his life long on the spot where midday had found him. But God has policemen on every street, and Mendel had sons in his house. The policemen came and put things in order. Day is day, and evening is evening. Everything is in order, Jews. Let's drink a glass of vodka."

Acceptance comes at a price. Arye-Leib reminds us of another man who tried to hold on to his passionate youth through love of

a young woman: "Strength thirsts," he comments on the tale of
King David and Bathsheba, "only sadness slakes the heart" (*I*, 360,
353). Life, he appears to be saying, is a wheel of desire. Only by
removing oneself from its incessant hungers can one find a measure
of peace. But Mendel obstinately refuses to loosen his grip on life.
When he finally does let go, he is sadder and perhaps wiser. Babel
often praised the joy of vigorous instinctual life, as he does in *Sunset*.
His work, however, is shadowed by the melancholy of a man who
stands somewhat apart from the world's bustle, musing, now ironically, now quizzically, over the confusions of the *comédie humaine*.

Maria

After writing *Maria* in 1933 Babel expressed fear that the play
would not accord with "the general party line,"[3] and subsequent
events proved him right: permission for production was granted and
then withdrawn. The play was entirely banned from the stage,
though it was published in 1935. In the preceding years the Soviet
Union had gone through the upheavals of the first Five Year Plan
and forced collectivization of the peasantry. Autonomous institutions and independent thought were ruthlessly extirpated. Writers
were expected to glorify the country's titanic struggle for industrialization. In literature purposeful, energetic heroes were the order
of the day. Through the example of his or her dedication, the positive
hero was to mobilize the will of the nation for the tasks of con-
structing a socialist society and protecting it from its enemies. Those
who opposed the collective purpose—subversives, laggards, weak-
lings and degenerates unable to break old bourgeois habits—were
to be rooted out and destroyed or, if their sins were venial, simply
ridiculed. The former was the solution of melodrama, the latter of
satire and the socialist comedy of manners. By an irony of history
the major literary genres of eighteenth-century absolutist society (to
satire and the comedy of manners we may add the panegyrical ode
in praise of the Great Leader) became the staples of "socialist
democracy."

The creative originality of *Sunset* was possible in the relative
freedom of the 1920s, when writers, though under severe pressure,
still enjoyed a degree of latitude, at least for formal experimentation.
By 1926, the year of its composition, the energies of the Russian
avant-garde were on the wane, but its aesthetic ideas had not yet

been proscribed. *Maria,* the product of a much darker era, is an idiosyncratic attempt on Babel's part to accommodate his work to the imperatives of "socialist" art. Set in the Civil War year of 1920, the play is peopled with the jaded aristocrats and speculating shysters who had been stock figures of the post-Revolutionary and NEP period, but by the mid-thirties were already anachronistic. Those totally alienated from the Soviet order had either been dealt with or else were so isolated as not to pose a threat. The conflicts of literature were now played out within the frame of a totalitarian society. It was no longer a question of "we" against "them," but of who is not fully, body and soul, one of "us." Babel could not overcome his fascination with an earlier period of Soviet history, when the new was still struggling to be born from the old. The most glaring oddity of *Maria,* however, is that its positive heroine, from whom the play takes its name, never once appears on stage.

In Russian literature—in Alexander Pushkin's *Eugene Onegin,* the novels of Ivan Goncharov and Ivan Turgenev, and again in Soviet drama of the thirties—women often prove to be the moral superiors of men. We do not see Maria, but we hear much about her in the talk of her disintegrating family, the Makovnins, and finally from her in a long letter read on stage. Her father is a former czarist general who plans to come to terms with the Bolsheviks but dies of a heart attack before succeeding. Her frivolous sister Lyudmila sinks into debauchery, while Katya, a family friend and retainer of sorts to these lost aristocrats, laments her inability to fill any place in the new society. The impotent ex-Prince Golitsyn, another associate of the Makovnins, escapes life by retreating into religious obscurantism. "What kind of home can this be—without children," the Makovnins' old nanny wonders. The Makovnins are a sterile family without a future. Already rootless, these declassé aristocrats have also become impoverished, and in their helpless dependency are exploited by an unscrupulous speculator, Isaac Dymshits, and his bizarre band of invalid crooks. Dymshits, who seems to have strayed into this somber play from the sunny pages of *Odessa Tales,* has been blessed with more than his share of Jewish wit, and his cynical epigrams provide some comic relief from the pained self-pity of the Mukovnins. "All the strength of the Mukovnins had gone into Maria," one character exclaims (*I,* 389, 382), and they all look to her for their salvation. She, however, has joined the Red Army and is off in the Ukraine preparing to fight the Poles. Perhaps

Babel kept her off stage out of an instinct that told him perfection is boring.

The play is stitched together from the fabric of melodrama. Poor Lyudmila is drugged, raped, infected with gonorrhea, and arrested. Shooting breaks out off-stage as the crooks flee from pursuing militia or fight among themselves. But the knot of a melodramatic plot is never tied. Dymshits and his weird cohorts remain pretty much in their sinister underworld, and the Mukovnins in their isolated apartment among memorabilia of another age. Incidents and images pile up cumulatively rather than in subordination to a controlling plot. The plot, such as it is, is resolved simply by General Mukovnin's dropping dead. The old order passes away and the new, represented by a young proletarian couple who move into the Mukovnins' family apartment, takes over. As in *Sunset,* time is Babel's true hero.

Maria is not a fully realized play, though it is not uninteresting either. Babel seems to have intended it as the first part of a trilogy that would cover the entire Soviet period (see *I,* 475). Many strings are left hanging: Dymshits simply fades away, we do not learn what happens to Lyudmila, Maria's adventures all lie in the future. The play has about it the sketchiness of the first stage in a larger design. The question of whether the surviving characters are complex enough to have sustained another two plays is moot.

The interesting aspect of *Maria* is the sense it conveys of a man struggling to come to terms with his historical situation. At a time when other writers were manufacturing uniform products on the assembly line of Soviet propaganda, Babel was still committed to making sense of the world. Though the Mukovnins are thin characters, relatives of the stereotypes of orthodox Soviet literature, their desperation comes through as genuine. Dymshits and his pals are brought into the play for the fun and fascination of black humor, but it is also through them that we hear about the Bolsheviks. The Soviet authority they know is the Soviet authority that really matters: the Cheka and the police. They give us a picture of a ruthless, hard lot. Their view is of course qualified by irony, since these are hardened criminals themselves. But since the Bolsheviks do not appear on stage to make their own case, the fear and resentment shown by these crooks (and most of the Mukovnin family) establish the climate in which the play's characters live.

At this moment of historical crisis, when the new is being painfully born from the old, Maria decides for the Bolsheviks. Described as a woman of compassion and strength, she enlists in the Revolution for the very same reasons her father, the ex-czarist general, is thinking of doing so. Nationalism and a wish to be on "the side of history," rather than Communist ideology, motivate both daughter and father. The Bolsheviks have won: by winning they have become, for better or worse, a manifestation of Russian destiny. To withdraw like Prince Golitsyn into religious passivity, or like Lyudmila into the self-indulgence of narcotics and sex, is to retreat from life. General Mukovnin sees the Bolsheviks as fulfilling the historical task of "gathering in the Russian lands" begun by the grand princes of medieval Muscovy. His hero is Peter the Great, who by the force of his powerful will molded the modern Russian state. Peter, says Mukovnin, taught that "to slow up the course of time is like dying." The Bolsheviks have infused Russian life with energy, another character proclaims, and father and daughter want to partake of that energy, refusing to wallow in the self-pity of the defeated. In her letter Maria writes of having finally escaped the isolation of that most European of Russian cities, St. Petersburg—"we lived there as in Polynesia." Traveling with the Red Army, she has for the first time in her sheltered life encountered the masses of Russian peasants and the variegated population of the Soviet Union—Cossack horsemen, Ukrainians, Tatars. She has visited ancient castles that have witnessed bloody battles of national survival, she has seen the awesome expanses of Russian space. In joining the Revolution she discovers authentic Russia (*I,* 370, 373, 384–86).

Many Russian intellectuals (and not only Russians) hopped on the bandwagon of Communism either out of conviction or out of an all-too-human desire to be on the side of power. Everyone likes a winner. The Russian intelligentsia, the great majority of whom derived from the gentry (and toward the end of the nineteenth century from the professional classes), had long felt guilty about its privileged isolation from the exploited Russian masses. For many— Alexander Blok is a notable example—accepting the Revolution was a path of repentance. Babel, however, had nothing to feel guilty about. He was a son of those oppressed masses, and of the most disenfranchised of them all, the Russian Jews. *Maria,* like the bulk of his work, shows a man making his choices with a clear head. In his art Babel refrains almost completely from sentimentalizing the world or his own personality. The Bolsheviks may or may not be as bad as Dymshits and his gruesome crew paint them, but nothing in the play indicates that living under their rule will be easy. Through the cardboard figure of Maria the play says yes to the Revolution as to a fait accompli, a determination of history. Babel chose to share the fate of his nation.

The only sentimental moment in the play comes in the upbeat ending, obligatory for orthodox Soviet writing. The working-class woman taking over the Mukovnin apartment is pregnant (a foil to the sterile Mukovnins); a worker polishing the floors in preparation for the new tenants comments that children born today "should be on time for a good life"; sunlight pours over a cleaning woman framed in a window "like a statue supporting the firmament, . . . against a spring sky." Though Babel had few if any illusions about the present, children gave him hope for the future. His Prince Golitsyn quotes the passage of Scripture, "Except a corn of wheat fall into the ground and die, it abideth alone but if it die, it brings forth much fruit." So much suffering and death, Babel felt, must surely issue in a new birth that would justify the price. To adhere to the old, to deny the reality of history, is to "abide alone." If this is self-delusion, it is of a common and understandable sort. Mukovnin is a rare bird among the Russian aristocracy, which was widely infected by the virus of anti-Semitism, for he admires Jews for their "energy, their life force, their power to resist" (I, 372). Babel identified the Revolution with life, despite his anxieties and misgivings. As the Jewish tradition untiringly teaches, he chose life, as he understood it, over death.

Films

The episodic structure of Babel's plays may have been influenced by the films, which were coming of age in the 1920s. Both plays cut rapidly from scene to scene, ranging over different settings. The theatricality of *Sunset* may also owe something to the movies. Like many films of the twenties—for example those of the great Sergey Eisenstein—it places an army of characters in scenes of public spectacle (the celebrations, the synagogue scene). And then from 1925 to the end of his career Babel worked on a wide range of screenplays for the burgeoning Soviet film industry. Among his many credits are several adaptations of his own stories, of works by Sholom Aleichem, a film about the notorious double agent Azef called *Lyotchiki*

(The aviators), now regarded as one of the best Soviet films of the 1930s, and a classic rendition of Turgenev's story "Bezhin Meadow." Several of Babel's screenplays have been published. Since a film is a collaboration of the narrative and visual arts, often including music as well, it is impossible to judge its merits from the screenplay alone. Read as "stories," however, Babel's scripts are not very interesting. *Benya Krik* (1926) draws upon "The King" and "How It Was Done in Odessa" of the *Odessa Tales*. The opening scenes, in the spirit both of the original stories and of film comedies of the 1920s, are filled with slapstick: the high incidence of women with mountainous breasts must have been a delight for the cameraman. Settings that Babel describes as "Dickensian" and "Hogarthian" provided opportunity for striking visual effects. The screenplay updates the stories by taking Benya into the post-Revolutionary period, when he joins the Bolsheviks, takes command of a regiment in the Red Army, and yet stubbornly persists in his ingrained habits. The difficulty of making oneself over was a common theme in the literature of the twenties (it is central to *Red Cavalry*, though less obviously so than in many other works of early Soviet literature). It is impossible to tell from the text whether Benya is sincere about reforming or merely using the Reds as a cover for his illicit activities, but the latter seems more likely. He is more true to his own character and undoubtedly more fun for the audience when throwing truck-drivers into the sea so he can steal their load of watermelons than he is when waving a red flag. At the end, the Bolsheviks gun him down as law and order triumph. Babel makes the ambush seem like a gratuitous murder.[4]

Bluzhdayushchie zvyozdy (Wandering stars, 1926), based on a Sholom Aleichem story, is unadulterated melodrama, the kind of thing upon which movies once throve. The film opens in a town of the pre-Revolutionary Pale of Settlement. Lyovushka Ratkovich is rich, talented, and unscrupulous; his girl friend Rachel is poor and pure. He abandons her for a career as a violinist, wins fame, fortune, and a ravishing countess to boot, and predictably slides into ruin as a drug addict and finally a suicide. She, after suffering insults as a Jew and the humiliation of being mistaken for a prostitute, finds salvation in the arms of the Social Democratic party and a revolutionary lover. At the conclusion the two of them turn their backs on decadent Europe and look ahead to the future in Russia.[5]

Staraya ploshchad, 4 (Old square, no. 4, written in 1939) is melodrama of another sort. A product of the post-Revolutionary period of Soviet history, its villains are no longer the West's jaded rich or conniving entrepreneurs but home-grown scoundrels. As the passions of the Revolutionary period faded, Soviet melodrama became domesticated, taking on the contours of the comedy of manners. Conflict, such as was tolerated, was "all in the family." Unable to examine social institutions or fundamental problems of human personality in a serious way, writers turned to describing quirks of character or errors of judgment that set off an individual from the accepted norm. The resulting literature was cheerfully pedagogical. Given the correct twist (usually administered by that deus ex machina of Soviet literature, the Communist party), villains were quickly reformed or at least rendered impotent, so that at the denouement the stage was filled with the one happy family that was the Soviet nation.

In *Old Square, No. 4* the good guys stand for initiative, teamwork, achievement, patriotism; the bad are scheming careerists, rigid pedants, and legalistic bureaucrats. The characters face the challenge of building a dirigible that will outperform its competition. Murashko, the head of the project, is a classic positive hero of socialist realist literature: tough yet compassionate, dedicated yet warm, uncompromising yet understanding. Above all, he recognizes no limits. If there is a job to be done, he will do it. His allies are the young (youth has a privileged position in modern totalitarian societies), his antagonists professors. Professor Polibin is a smooth talker and a "theoretician of the first water." Professor Talmazov goes by the book, and foreign ones at that! Murashko, the blunt man of action, stakes his money on the eccentric Zhukov, "a dreamer and a self-taught man," as designer of the dirigible USSR-1. Zhukov may have his oddities but he also has vision, a dream of eventually designing an airship to fly to the moon. He dismisses the conventional wisdom of academic scientists as akin to religious obscurantism. Like Murashko, he is selfless. Unsullied by careerist ambitions, he only wishes to see Soviet dirigibles fly. The dirigible does fly but it cannot land. The error in the design is discovered, but Professor Polibin shows up with an order to cease operations (Talmazov has in the meanwhile seen the error of his ways); the young enthusiasts of the Comsomol (the Communist Youth Organization) stage a fire, which, according to the regulations, is an emergency taking precedence over Polibin's restraining order. Murashko gives the command and the Soviet dirigible indeed does fly (and lands!). Everyone celebrates. Murashko, whose life is all work and no play, is quickly off on another mission, producing high altitude bombers.

To those uninitiated in the Byzantine convolutions of Soviet ideology the screenplay may seem to defend individualism against conformity, for the bold Murashko and the visionary inventor Zhukov, a stock romantic figure, are vindicated in their struggle with the hidebound academics. Russians would not make that mistake. Murashko leaves no doubt that he speaks and acts for the Party. Attacks on routine-bound bureaucrats are even today a routine feature of the Soviet press. Far from glorifying the individual, the function of such Stalinist literature has been to discredit all institutions that might stand between him and the state. Unhindered by the disciplines of academic science and the restraints of cultural traditions, the new Soviet man, like Murashko, knows no limits.[6] He can do anything. But, stripped of any ideology or values opposed to those of the state, he can also be ordered to do anything. Babel probably composed this pap simply to make money or establish his political reliability. To his credit, he did soften the edges. When Talmazov's graduate student ominously mentions the NKVD as perhaps the proper agency to handle Zhukov, Murashko intervenes with the reminder that everyone on the project is engaged in the work of the Party. Any disagreements are on the level of a family squabble.[7]

Chapter Nine

The Life of Art: Three Stories

The role of art and the artist always troubled Babel. Even when his work is about other things—Jewish life in Odessa, war and revolution, growing up—that theme lies under the surface. Like many modern artists, he has become a problem to himself. He can no longer take for granted what he is doing, the activity of writing; rather, he must understand and justify it.

The *Odessa Tales* are not very kind to the occupation of writer. The stories are an exercise in self-parody, mocking this futile observer of the doings of others, "with spectacles on his nose and autumn in his heart." He merely records while passionate men like Benya Krik act: "Passion," not reflection, "rules the universe." The writer is doomed to sit on a cemetery wall among the dead, watching the deeds of the living. Ever since Plato in the *Phaedrus* decried the value of writing in written words of great beauty, such arguments have tended to cancel themselves in paradox. We are told of the artist's impotence in works that demonstrate his powers. Silence would be more consistent. But then, as is true of many forms of self-denigration, that of the *Odessa Tales* conceals a latent assertion of superiority. No matter how much Babel may praise and envy Benya, the act of creation gives him precedence over his creature. Benya acts, but we never forget that Babel is pulling the strings.

In *Red Cavalry* passionate men ride into history to reshape the world. As witness to the onset of revolutionary changes in the character of human life, Babel posed more complex questions than those of his earlier cycle: What price do men pay for severing their ties to traditional values? Are there passive as well as active virtues? Do suffering, compassion, and reflection possess powers as essential for the formation of a man or woman as the capacity for heroic action? Can human beings exist in a wilderness without the nourishment of art or the hopes of prophecy? Painfully sensitive to the contradictions of human life, the Babel of *Red Cavalry* sought to balance the demands history makes upon men to act, even violently, with the human need for compassion and the solace of art.

In the *Dovecot* cycle Babel comes down as hard as ever on Jewish passivity. The sight of his fictional father's fawning submissiveness, the pressures placed upon him by his father's compensatory ambitions, wound the boy deeply and cause him to look for other values on which to build his life. Quite unlike the self-deprecating narrator of the *Odessa Tales*, he finds in art a way out of personal humiliation and Jewish victimization. Art, like action, is power. It is the power to name things, which he learns from Nikitich, the guardian angel of Jewish waifs; the power to make things, which he discovers in Trottyburn's brother's lovingly crafted pipes. Poetry, Yeats declared, grows out of an argument, not with another, but with oneself. Babel's lifelong struggle to come to terms with his profession was also a struggle to discover who he was. He admired and even envied the movers and shakers of this world. Like Marianne Moore, he worried of poetry that "there are things that are important beyond all this fiddle." But also, like his American compeer, he knew that he would find in it "a place for the genuine" if he searched hard enough.

"Line and Color"

"Liniya i tsvet" (Line and color), the title of a story Babel published in 1923, might stand as a subtitle for his entire oeuvre, especially *Red Cavalry,* where a variegated and brilliantly hued imagery is contained in the tight contours of a highly controlled syntax. This allegorical tale assumes the form of a debate in which the future head of the revolutionary Provisional Government, Alexander Kerensky, takes the side of color; the first-person narrator, that of line. (Babel had met Kerensky at a sanatorium in Finland before the Revolution, in 1916.) The two men go for a walk in the woods, where the narrator discovers that Kerensky, who is nearsighted but refuses to wear glasses, cannot see the landscape he moves in. However, Kerensky considers it a point of honor to be blind to the world. Like the young man of the earlier story "Inspiration" (or like a caricature of a symbolist poet), he is a solipsist enjoying the emanations of his own imagination. He needs only formless impressions of color in order to construct a world for himself: "I don't need your line, as vulgar as reality. You live no better than a teacher of

trigonometry, while I'm enveloped by wonders. . . . What do I
need Finnish clouds for, when above my head I see a glowing ocean?
What do I need line for when I have color? For me the whole world
is a gigantic theater. . . ."

But line draws boundaries and makes objects perceptible. Beauty,
the narrator argues, lies not in vague impressions that stimulate the
mind's random imaginings, but in the forms of things seen with
exactitude: "Line, that divine trait, mistress of the world [*vlastitel-
nitsa mira*], has forever escaped you. Here we are, you and I, walking
about in this garden of enchantments. . . . All our lives we shall
never see anything more beautiful. And you can't see the pink edges
of the frozen waterfall, over there by the stream! You are blind to
the Japanese chiseling of the weeping willow leaning over the
waterfall."

The story ends with one of those Babelian codas that so often
elevate the narrative to a new level of meaning. The scene moves
ahead a year to the turbulent days of June 1917, when mass demonstrations of workers and soldiers sympathetic to the Bolsheviks
greeted the first All-Soviet Congress, presaging the failed coup d'état
of July and the eventually successful overthrow of the Provisional
Government in October. Kerensky addresses the restive mob, but
as he is shortsighted he cannot perceive its true character and appeals
to vague abstractions of Russia as "mother and wife." Trotsky follows
him to the podium and "in an implacable voice" opens his speech:
"Comrades." Here the story breaks off. The rest is history.[1]

The point is clear. Trotsky can see—the mood of the workers,
the demands of the political situation—and hence the path to power
is open to him. To perceive the real is the first step in achieving
power. But Babel conveys a certain sympathy for Kerensky's position, which blurs the schematic dichotomies of his allegory. Kerensky is blind, yet he too, like the narrator, sees beauty, even if
only the illusory beauty of the mind's contrivings. Isn't art after all
a happy coincidence of perception and imagination, of apprehended
realities and subjective musings, of line *and* color? Writers of the
twenties, products of a revolutionary epoch, often assumed a posture
of hardheaded toughness toward what they viewed as the sentimen-
talities of bourgeois culture. Kerensky is the victim of his excessively
emotional sensibility, but the narrator's insistence upon austere line
and reality to the detriment of color and imagination does not accord
with Babel's own practice. Pan Apolek of *Red Cavalry,* Babel's model

of the artist, comes closer to the mark. Though Apolek finds the starting point of his art in the real world about him—the ordinary sinners of the village of Novograd—through the creative act he transforms them according to the dictates of his personal vision.

"Di Grasso"

The relation of art to reality is mysterious. Art opens our eyes to the world around us and frees us from the blinders of unseeing habit, but it does so in unexpected ways.

In "Di Grasso" (1937) the usual opera tour to theater-hungry Odessa has flopped. A Sicilian dramatic company headed by the tragedian Di Grasso is invited to fill the gap and opens the season with a corny folk pastoral that threatens to be as disastrous as the failed opera. But Di Grasso, who is playing a lovesick shepherd scorned by a peasant maiden who prefers the blandishments of a city slicker, saves the day. As the hackneyed plot drags on into the third act, Di Grasso suddenly performs an awesome leap across the stage, falls upon his rival, and pretends to bite through the latter's neck. The audience is bowled over and the play is a smash. In ensuing performances the gifted Di Grasso confirms "with every word and movement that there is more justice and hope in the frenzy of noble passion than in all the joyless rules of the world."

As almost always in a Babel story the narrator is the true protagonist: it is he who learns and changes. In "Di Grasso" he is Babel at fourteen, who has been hustling theater tickets for some extra cash. Like the boy of the *Dovecot* cycle, he feels trapped in life's entanglements. He has secretly pawned his father's gold watch to an unscrupulous speculator in theater tickets, who, though he has gotten his money back, refuses to return it. Knowing the characters of both his father and his employer, he expects no mercy: "Hemmed in by these people, I watched how the hoops of others' happiness rolled past me."

Through Di Grasso's leap he rediscovers his happiness. Di Grasso's performance far exceeds what ordinary people do or expect their neighbors to do, and yet in performing the extraordinary, he inspires others to perceive the ordinary in a new light. Leaving the theater, the boy discovers a changed world: "With a clarity such as I had never before experienced, I saw the columns of the Municipal Building soaring up into the heights, the illuminating foliage of the boulevard, Pushkin's bronze head touched by the dim gleam of the moon, saw for the first time the things surrounding me as they really were—frozen in silence and ineffably beautiful."

Art is a paradoxical act of transcendence. It goes beyond the ordinary only to renew it, takes us away from the usual so that we may find our way back to it, "estranges" us only to bring us home.[2] The key to this puzzling paradox is freedom. Recognizing in Di Grasso's performance the possibility of freedom, the boy along with the rest of the audience can also, if but for a moment, throw off the shackles of habit and routine—"all the joyless rules of the world" that keep people from taking pleasure in the immediate experience of reality. Perception is not an automatic faculty. It is a volitional act that requires the space of freedom for its fullest exercise. The people chained in Plato's cave—that classic metaphor of the human condition—cannot turn their heads to see the true reality of things. For Babel art provides a jolt that frees us to see the world as it really is: sometimes tragically painful, and sometimes, as in "Di Grasso," "ineffably beautiful."

"Guy de Maupassant"

"Guy de Maupassant" (1932) is a masterful story, Babel at his best. In a way it is a reprise of "In the Basement," an expansion of that story's satire on the Jewish nouveau riche. However, the protagonist (Babel again) has outgrown his adolescent embarrassment over his family's social and economic deficiencies. He is now a young man, embarked on his career as a writer. In art he has discovered a value to oppose to the gross materialism and complacent self-satisfaction of the bourgeoisie.

It is 1916. The young writer has come north to St. Petersburg and made his home among struggling artists like himself, men "flung out of the round of ordinary life." Rejecting the envy-ridden ambitions of his father, he has opted to follow in the footsteps of his eccentric and rebellious grandfathers: "Better starve, go to jail, or become a bum than spend ten hours every day behind a desk in an office. . . . The wisdom of my grandfathers was firmly implanted in my head: we are born to enjoy our work, our fights, and our love. . . ." To support himself he accepts a position assisting a wealthy dilletante, Raisa Benderskaya, in translating Maupassant. The Benderskys are converted Jews, people without familial or ethnic ties (*bez rodu i plemeni*), who have struck it rich. Alienated from their past, without vital connections to a living community, they have turned into materialistic sensualists for whom art is a luxurious adornment or an amusing diversion. "The money made by their shrewd husbands," Babel writes, "is transformed by these women into a pink layer of fat on the belly, on the nape of the neck, on well-rounded shoulders. Their subtle sleepy smiles drive officers from the local garrison crazy. 'Maupassant,' Raisa said to me, 'is the only passion of my life.' "

At the center of the story is a marvelously comic seduction scene, when the fumbling youth falls for the luscious Raisa to the accompaniment of a reading of Maupassant's "L'Aveu." As the coachman of the story comes closer to the object of his desires, the young writer approaches his. Babel turns into Polyte imploring his coy but ultimately agreeable Céleste "to have some fun." However, when finally ready to make his move, he drunkenly stumbles against the bookshelf knocking over Maupassant's collected works, "twenty-nine volumes, twenty-nine shells stuffed with pity, genius, and passion."

These passions of art are set against the bourgeois passions for accumulation and conspicuous consumption. The young writer returns from the ornate Bendersky mansion to his dingy flat among the artists and intellectuals of the capital's Bohemia, where he picks up Edouard Maynial's biography of Maupassant, a grim story of a lifelong struggle of creativity and joy against the ravages of congenital syphilis: headaches, hypochondria, weakening sight, attempted suicide, and finally madness. The end found Maupassant, once successful and celebrated, crawling about on his knees in an asylum, devouring his own excrement. The last line in his hospital report read: "Monsieur de Maupassant va s'animaliser" (M. de Maupassant is going to turn into an animal).

This is the stuff of sentimentalism—poor, doomed artist suffers while the obtuse bourgeoisie prosper. But the story is anything but sentimental. The trick is style, as Babel told Paustovsky (and he again tells Raisa, who can only manage a wooden lifeless prose). Style makes the story a masterpiece. The Benderskys come to life in a richly opulent and deliciously comic language that says more than a thousand moral strictures. Maupassant's horrible ordeal, by contrast, is narrated as a matter-of-fact, clinical account without an iota of false pathos. Babel certainly wants to make a point, "to say something," but, like all superior writers, he wishes first of all to present a world.

That world is a puzzling and uncertain place. The Benderskys' greatest fault lies not in their mindless pursuit of wealth and the trappings of culture—in this they are merely silly—but in their isolation from their fellowman. In the figure of Maupassant Babel discovers something never dreamed of in their philosophy. "Di Grasso" and "Guy de Maupassant" form a pair. In both tales the activity of the artist embraces values that all of us can attain but that too often escape us in the ordinary bustle of life's getting and losing. Di Grasso's leap is the leap of freedom that is the essence of creative action. Maupassant exemplifies courageous dedication in the face of enormous suffering. If art is joy, it is also pain. Literature opens us to the soul of the other. The Benderskys have shut themselves up in a gilded cage but human suffering descends in a black cloud to overshadow their trivial pursuits. Maupassant's ordeal is terrible and inexplicable, for there is no logical or moral reason for such suffering, no balancing of the scales to justify it. Yet men and women do suffer so. The narrator's final attitude is right. Before such suffering one can only pause in awe and respect: "I read the book to the end and got out of bed. The fog came close to the window and hid the universe from me. My heart contracted as the foreboding of some essential truth touched me."

Chapter Ten
Last Works (1928–38)
Writers in Uniform

The announcement of the First Five Year Plan in 1928 marked the beginning of difficult years for Soviet writers and the Soviet people. In retrospect, the period of Lenin's New Economic Policy or NEP (1921–27) would appear as a respite between revolutionary storms and the terrors of Stalinism. Through the mid-twenties there existed a free sector of the economy; peasants, though without legal right to land, still enjoyed the free use of it; a measure of cultural independence was tolerated. The consolidation of Stalin's power changed Russia from a dictatorship to a totalitarian state. Under the Five Year Plan peasants were forcibly herded into state-controlled collectives, and industrialization was scheduled at a breakneck pace. The economic consequences were mixed. Consumer goods were scarcer than in the NEP period, while basic industry grew rapidly. In a remarkably brief time Russia changed from an agricultural country into a modern industrial state, but at enormous human cost. Workers were driven to the limits of their endurance; injuries were common, many died. The peasants furiously resisted confiscation of lands they had over the course of Russian history regarded as their own. They left vast areas of arable soil untilled, and slew their livestock rather than turn them over to the despised collectives, or else simply to avoid starvation. Famine reached epidemic proportions. Those who rebelled were arrested and deported to concentration camps in the arctic zone and the eastern regions. Joining them were masses of peasants, the so-called *kulaks,* whose only crime was that they were somewhat better off than their impoverished neighbors. The government encouraged a "class" war in the countryside, setting the poorer peasants against the more successful. Victims of hunger, destitution, and state violence numbered in the millions.

In effect the Soviet people became the property of the state, though the extent to which they have preserved their humanity in the face of brutal oppression and enormous suffering is often not fully appreciated. Any vestige of political, social, economic, or cultural autonomy surviving from the twenties was ruthlessly exterminated. In a society conceived as an army, artists were no different from other recruits: they were viewed as "shock workers" in the task of "socialist construction," and were expected to boost public morale. A puffed-up journalism became the order of the day; anything resembling personal feeling or imaginative thought was suspect. The Russian Association of Proletarian Writers (RAPP), which gained ascendancy over the literary profession in 1929, demanded a documentary "literature of fact" in which the "facts" were known even before they were perceived. In the twenties RAPP and the proletarian organizations that preceded it had to contend with other groups with other views, some also Communist, some formed by ideologically uncommitted "fellow travelers." During the course of the Five Year Plan the quarrels came to an end. First RAPP destroyed its competitors, and then the Party, which would brook no independence even from its allies, destroyed RAPP.

As part of its attempt to create a monolithic society, the state herded writers into a single organization, the Union of Soviet Writers, whose members were obliged to profess a single aesthetic, social realism. In this oxymoron the "realist" half has been generally understood as an aping of the techniques of nineteenth-century fiction— Tolstoy remains the supreme model—though, if it contains the correct message, even a work of fantasy may be regarded as "realistic." The "socialist" half has meant whatever the Communist party at a given moment wishes it to mean. Andrey Zhdanov, the government spokesman at the Union's first Congress in 1934, spoke of the hybrid nature of socialist realism, its wedding of realistic form with the content of a specific political ideology, as follows: "Truthfulness and historical concreteness of artistic depiction must be combined with the task of ideological remolding and re-education of the toiling people in the spirit of socialism. . . . Soviet literature must know how to portray our heroes, it must be able to look into our tomorrow."[1] Realism of the nineteenth century, taking the natural sciences as its model, saw itself as an experiential mode of inquiry into the nature of reality. The avant-garde of modernism, like Marxism, had its eyes on the future, but it insisted upon a pluralistic, experimental spirit in creative action. For socialist realism the future is a given, and the artist is reduced to a performer, a trained seal dancing to somebody else's tune. Free experimentation in form and free exploration of a subject matter had begun to disappear in the late twenties; by the thirties they were for most a memory, or else, for the few who persevered, a source of peril.

Babel virtually ceased publishing from 1926 through 1930, and when he resumed in 1931 he turned out relatively little.[2] That he maintained his proclaimed "genre of silence" in face of the pressures on a Soviet writer merely to produce is a measure of his integrity. Even more impressive is the quality of the work he did turn out in those years of strict censorship and ominous warnings to writers who did not toe the line. The thirties saw the completion of the very fine *Dovecot* cycle, such unquestionable masterpieces as "Guy de Maupassant" and "Di Grasso," and several other stories of merit. Even when he tried to conform to the required stereotypes, as in the play *Maria,* he still injected life into their cast-iron molds. As a youth he had vowed commitment to his art. He kept that promise.

A Writer in Crisis

Babel encountered enormous obstacles in his quest to find himself as a man and a writer. It is perhaps idle to speculate what he might have achieved had the culture he lived in evolved differently. Not given to wishful thinking, he fully accepted the burdens history had placed on his shoulders. Still, the nature of his talent might have presented difficulties even in a more tolerant place and time. "I started writing as a youth," he said in an interview of 1937, "then stopped for a number of years, then wrote in a torrent for several years, then stopped again." "I am the sort of writer," he wrote a friend in 1928, "who has to keep silent for several years so as then to explode."[3] The torrent flowed for about five years—1921 through 1925—when Babel's essential corpus was written or begun: *Odessa Tales, Red Cavalry,* two of the four stories that make up the *Dovecot* cycle, "The Story of My Dovecot" and "First Love." A number of his later stories were actually, according to Babel's dating on the manuscripts, begun in the early twenties. Others (as well as the play *Sunset*), though not so dated, revert to familiar themes and places of *Odessa Tales* and *Red Cavalry,* or revive the style of those earlier works. After 1925 Babel felt himself at an impasse: he was going to the desk drawer for unfinished business or to memory for old subjects. His career recalls Gogol's, a writer whom he resembles in other ways as well. In each case a great outburst of creativity flashes like a comet across the sky and then is quickly extinguished. Babel, though he wrote well after 1925, never duplicated the achievement of *Red Cavalry*. Like every major talent he wanted to produce another "big book"—whether a cycle of stories, a novel, or a series of plays—but a sustained body of work eluded him. He despaired of his inability to publish regularly, but the "torrent" of creative energy he seemed to require refused to come. In the thirties it dwindled to an occasional autumn shower.

Part of the problem was his style. Babel reached his peak in the heyday of Russian "ornamentalism," when post-Revolutionary writers continued the symbolist effort to poeticize prose. Babel, with one foot in the tradition of the ironically pointed French *conte*, was able to blend lyricism into finely structured stories, but he and his contemporaries had difficulty mastering longer narrative forms. Their art was an art of the miniature. Lyrical, metaphoric, decorative, the prose of the early twenties could do anything except sustain a plot of magnitude. When novels were attempted, they tended, like Boris Pilnyak's *Goly god* (Naked year, 1922), to break down into poetic fragments. Working in the manner of Bely and other symbolists, the ornamentalists substituted myth for the social entanglements that require the breadth of the novel to work themselves out. Since human beings have a need for stories as much as poetic vision, it was not a manner that could long prevail.

As early as 1925—before *Red Cavalry* had even appeared in book form—Babel wrote Gorky that he considered his own works "artificial and florid." "I have a thirst to write long," he wrote his editors in 1929. Through the thirties he talked of projects for novels, even undertook a few, but nothing came of it. Once *Sunset* and *Maria* were under his belt, he decided to become a playwright: "A strange change has come over me," he said. "I don't feel like writing in prose. I want to use only the dramatic form." He was looking not only for new genres but for a new style: "My transfer to new literary rails," he wrote in 1928, "is giving me trouble. The professional pursuit of literature (and here [in Paris] I am for the first time pursuing it as a professional) is giving me trouble." "It is much more difficult for me to work than before," he wrote in another letter of the same year. "I have different demands, different methods—and I want to move on to another 'class' (as they say of boxers and horses)—the class of quiet, subtle, and not trivial, writing."[4]

Artists tend to be perfectionists, and we should not take Babel's self-disparagement too seriously. But in what sense had he not been a "professional" previously? He had after all produced some of the best short stories in the history of Russian literature, and won wide recognition. Perhaps "professional" was merely a code word for a dutiful Soviet writer-bureaucrat, and Babel despaired of the necessity, imposed by the hardening political situation, of turning himself into one of that tribe. But there is another sense (by no means belittling) in which Babel was not a "professional" writer. Not only is his style lyrical, but so is his impulse to expression. His work is not strictly autobiographical—perhaps no fiction ever is—but it is autobiographical in spirit. Babel's true subject is himself in the process of discovering the world. Except for occasional ethnographic sketches, his oeuvre is an unfolding bildungsroman. His creative energies draw their inspiration from that great emotional upheaval in every person's life—the passage from youth to maturity—which has been the motive of much of modern literature. Though subjective in nature, his work is by no means an exercise in narcissistic indulgence. He views the self critically, distances it through irony, and allows "the other"—Jewish gangster, pious Hasid, Russian Cossack—his own claims. His stories describe collisions between a searching self and a complex world, itself torn by conflict. These confrontations—of the self and the other, the old and the new, Jew and Gentile—are not developed in sociological extension or psychological depth in the manner of the nineteenth-century novel, but are perceived lyrically and symbolically. Of Babel's first two books, *Odessa Tales*, in its attempt to paint the *comédie humaine* of Moldavanka's Jewry, is closer to the designs of naturalistic fiction. But its colors are too flamboyant to be confused with drab reality, its characters too comically fantastical to be taken for ordinary human beings. It is not what they mean to themselves but what they mean to the narrator—the young intellectual with spectacles on his nose and autumn in his heart—that ultimately interests Babel. The role of the mediating narrator is even stronger in *Red Cavalry*, where he is a character in the action. A turbulent universe becomes grist for the ever-turning mill of his reflections. Chance encounters, violent eruptions, incongruities of existence lead the mind to revelations, lyrical epiphanies of the mysterious nature of the things. History

is the subject of *Red Cavalry* but, except for the process of education
the hero-narrator undergoes, its procedure is nonhistorical. A world
does not evolve; it is instead evoked through portentous imagery,
fragments of experience, sudden flashes of illumination.

When Babel spoke of abandoning his "artificial and florid style"
and moving on to the class of "quiet, clear writing," he had in
mind giving up ornamentalism. Poetic prose no longer satisfied
him, and besides it had gone out of fashion. Lenin's New Economic
Policy brought about the relative stability the novel requires, and
in the mid-twenties it made a comeback: Konstantin Fedin's *Goroda
i gody* (Cities and years) appeared in 1924, Leonid Leonov's *Barsuki*
(The badgers) in 1925 and *Vor* (The thief) in 1927, Yury Olesha's
Zavist (Envy) in 1927, the first three volumes of Mikhail Sholokhov's
massive *Tikhy Don* (The quiet Don) between 1928 and 1933. In
the *Dovecot* cycle, begun in 1925, Babel had already started to
develop a fuller narrative manner, moving away from his lyrical
style and perhaps also from his lyrical orientation on the self. A
writer (like the rest of us), if he does not wish to stagnate, cannot
dwell on the saga of growing up forever. A "professional" writer
publishes regularly, and this may be all Babel had in mind. He also
can handle a wide range of material. Writing plays was one way to
take himself out of his writing, and he does not appear as a character
in the unfinished cycle of stories he began on the collectivization
of the peasants (which may have been intended as a novel), and in
several of his later stories his role is significantly reduced. In the
thirties Babel exhibited the waverings of a man who knows he cannot
continue in the old ways but has not discovered the new. When
not dragging dusty manuscripts and familiar ideas out of his port-
folio, he tried his hand at something different—novels, which he
could not complete, and plays. In search of new forms, he was also
searching for new themes, but did not find them. When he made
a breakthrough to a work of exceptional distinction, as in "Awakening," "Guy de Maupassant," and "Di Grasso," it was to add
another chapter to his continuing tale of coming of age. Perhaps
Babel was the sort of writer—there have been many—who could
not pass beyond the crisis of youth. The times he lived in did not
make things any easier. That was his dilemma as he described it to
Ervin Sinkó: his silence was suspect, but if he went his own way,
the consequences might be even more dangerous.[5]

On "Social Command"

Either because he was required to or because he thought it the wise thing to do, Babel in 1930 joined the army of writers sent off as recruits to industrial sites and collective farms to sing the glories of socialist construction. The assignment was not unwelcome, since he hoped to find there the new subjects he needed. He visited several collective farms in the Ukraine and the huge steel plant at Dnepropetrovsk. Two sketches from a projected work on collectivization have survived, though whether they were intended as parts of a novel or another cycle of stories is unclear. "Gapa Guzhva" was published in 1931; "Kolyvushka" posthumously.[6] Babel was nobody's fool. He certainly realized what was going on, but at most he could only hint at the realities. That both surviving pieces are honest journeyman's work, free of cant and overt propaganda, is praise enough, considering the times.

The two pieces are ethnographic sketches describing the countryside in process of collectivization. The style is subdued and factual, the dialogue filled with Ukrainianisms. Now and then Babel indulges in an ornamental image, which can be jarring, for his more lush manner depended on the presence of a sophisticated narrator, while in these stories he effaced himself (they are told in the third person).

Fictions are curious things. If a character intended to be perceived negatively is allowed to dominate the narrative, he will usually win a measure of our sympathy. Dostoevsky's "underground man" is mean and nasty, but we side with him much of the time that he excoriates the hypocrisies of respectable society. Gapa Guzhva is a wild spirit, a female and gentile Benya Krik. We encounter her in the middle of an orgy, celebrating six weddings in "the ways of old times." Her greatest worry is the fate of the whores under the new order. She (and presumably her kind) have exhausted the representative of the District Executive Committee for collectivization, who is replaced by a trouble shooter, a no-nonsense judge nicknamed Two-Hundred-and-Sixteen-Percent for the quota of grain he was able to squeeze out of another village. Upon arriving in Velikaya Krinitsa he refuses to call a general meeting, as was the practice of his predecessors, preferring to see to things himself. If we had any doubts, matters are now clear. The so-called "collective" is a creation of the police. Gapa submits to the judge's promise of a better life.

The last sentence reads: "Silence spread over Velikaya Krinitsa, over the flat, grave-like, icy desert of the village night." Even when he was under pressure to compose panegyrics, Babel's imagination was more haunted by the death of the old than excited by the birth of the new.

"Kolyvushka," also named after its central character, is about a man who fights back. In despair at losing his house, expelled from the community for arrears in taxes, Kolyvushka kills his mare, who is with foal, and smashes a seeding machine. The description of the killing is a strong piece of writing, precise and finely detailed: "With hunched shoulders he jerked out the axe, held it up in the air for a moment and struck the horse on the head. One of its ears jerked back, the other twitched and lay flat. The mare groaned and bolted. The sledge turned over and wheat scattered in curved lines over the snow. The horse reared up with its forelegs in the air and its head thrown back. Beside one of the sheds it got caught up in the teeth of a harrow. Its eyes appeared from under a veil of pouring blood and it whinnied plaintively. The foal stirred inside it and a vein swelled up on its belly."

"I am a man," Kolyvushka protests. Babel leaves the attitudes of the other villagers hazy, but in reality thousands were engaged in a similarly futile rebellion. That his accuser at a meeting of the Village Council is a foul-mouthed, vicious hunchback calling for blood does not, however, endear his enemies to the reader. The story ends with Kolyvushka, a broken man, his hair turned white with grief, walking off into the lonely distance.

As far as we know nothing came of Babel's trip to Dnepropetrovsk, but in 1934 he did publish a piece of "production fiction." "Neft" (Oil) has all the ingredients of a socialist realist potboiler, except the uplift. The characters are there, only the message is uncertain. Leading the cast of stock figures is the tough-talking narrator, Klavdiya (the story is in the form of a letter). Klavdiya is the office head of the Oil Syndicate and a hard-as-nails "new woman" of the Soviet era—competent, determined, without illusions. Assorted holdovers from the old regime are brought in for contrast: a pedantic professor who doubts the capacity of the Syndicate to meet production norms, a genteel ex-aristocrat too scrupulous to bear her child out of wedlock. To the former our heroine mouths a standard cliché of the era: "We reject the multiplication table as a guide to statesmanship." The new Soviet hero, like Murashko of *Old Square*,

No. 4, knows no limits either of nature or logic. To her pregnant friend, she responds with characteristic hardboiled unsentimentality: "Other days, other ways. We'll manage without [a husband]." Klavdiya eventually turns out to have a heart of gold under her rhinoceros hide. This is by no means a violation of the canons of socialist realism. The hero is perfect. Lest he come across as a machine, the author introduces certain harmless foibles to show him as human, and hence even more perfect.

Curiously, not the production of oil but of a child is at issue in "Oil." The story poses the usual question of the genre: Will the Syndicate heroically meet the challenge of outstripping its production norms? But that is incidental. Instead this miniature soap opera turns on the question of whether Zina will have her baby. After a hysterical fit of the sort spoiled ex-aristocrats are supposed to indulge in, she resolves to go ahead with it. Everyone is happy, including tough Klavdiya. Children were very much on Babel's mind in the thirties. He had fathered a daughter in 1929. The idiocies and brutalities of the present made him look to the future for hope.

Farewell to Odessa

The earlier "Karl-Yankel" (1931) is an expression of that hope. The hyphenated name belongs to an infant. "Karl" is after Marx; "Yankel" is of course Yiddish. The hope is that traditional Jewish culture and the new Soviet order will find a bond, like the hyphen, to glue them together. The story takes place in Odessa, but it differs from *Odessa Tales.* In line with Babel's intention to move into a period of "quiet, clear" writing, the manner, though still comic, avoids the verbal play and fanciful whimsicality of the earlier cycle. The characters are funny, but they are real people, not cartoons. The narrative conventions are closer to those of realistic fiction, as a detailed family history is followed by a dramatic scene during which the issues of the plot come to a head.

Yoyna Brutman is a puny, timid blacksmith with an Odessan love for wine. His wife is a large and powerful woman, and also a pious Hasid. Their sons have inherited her strength but not her religious beliefs. Two of them are a new breed of Jew, "tough fighting men" of the Revolution. A lone daughter, Polina, shares her father's timidity. Polina marries a dedicated Communist, but when they have a son Polina's mother kidnaps him to have him

circumcised and named Yankel instead of Karl. She is brought to
trial, along with the circumciser. The description of the latter,
Naftula Gerchuk, is the most negative portrait of a Jew in all of
Babel's work (was Babel trying to score points with the anti-religious
authorities?), but still, at the trial he shows himself capable of a
witty Jewish cynicism that is not without charm.

The Prosecutor thundered from the dais, endeavoring to prove that the
little surgeon was the servant of a cult. . . .
    "Were you not surprised by the arrival of Citizeness Brutman at a late
hour, in the rain, with a new born child in her arms?"
    "I am surprised," replied Naftula, "when a human being does something
in a human way, but when he just plays the fool, then I'm not surprised."

The trial is a comic oasis in this didactic tale. Russia in the twenties
was a backward country in the birth pains of modernization, and
the spontaneous ways of uneducated provincials caught up in the
machine of impersonal bureaucratic institutions provided a natural
source of comedy, as in the works of Zoshchenko, Ilf and Petrov,
and Zamyatin.

"Tell us witness, Did you know of your husband's decision to call the
child Karl?"
    "I did."
    "What name did your mother give him?"
    "Yankel."
    "And you, witness, what did you call your son?"
    "I called him 'sweety pie.' "
    "What was your motive in calling him 'sweety pie'?"
    "I call all children 'sweety pie.' "

Little Karl-Yankel disrupts these solemn proceedings by bawling,
and Babel takes advantage of the interruption for a concluding
thought. Surveying the motley crowd of court officials, bright-eyed
Comsomols, and Galician *tsaddiks* (holy men) come from Poland to
defend the Jewish faith, he reflects: "From the window flew recti-
linear streets trodden by my childhood and youth. . . . I had grown
up on these streets, and now it was Karl-Yankel's turn. But they
hadn't fought for me as they were now fighting for him, there were
few to whom I was of any concern. 'It's not possible,' I whispered
to myself, 'that you won't be happy, Karl-Yankel. It's not possible

that you won't be happier than I.' " The effect of this passage may very well depend on the reader's politics. If one believes (or believed) that there really existed a community of interest among religious traditionalists, Communist idealists, and bureaucratic functionaries, then the squabbles over Karl-Yankel's fate may seem merely a temporary traffic jam on the highway of inevitable progress, and the ending will be stirring. If not, it may read as wishful thinking.

Two other stories that take the Odessa saga into the post-Revolutionary years are written in a mood of elegiac nostalgia. Babel takes leave of the world in which he had grown up, the culture that had nourished him, the characters whose escapades he had relished. Tinged by sadness at the passing of things, the two tales are yet quite unsentimental. In keeping with the stoic character of his work, Babel accepts history as fact. The clock has moved ahead and there is no turning it back.

Though the lyrical exuberance and playfulness that marked his earlier writings faded with the passage of time, "Konets bogadel'ni" (The end of the old folk's home, 1932) still has much of the old Babelian fun about it.[7] The enterprising Jews of an old folk's home discover a way to flourish in the midst of post-Revolutionary famine. Lady Luck and the Goddess of Irony have given them a coffin, and a shortage of lumber allows them to seize a monopoly of the burial business. Reviving a forgotten Jewish law that declares that a coffin should not come between the worms and their appointed task ("From the earth thou camest, and to the earth thou shalt return"), they reuse it for each funeral ceremony, dumping their successive clients into the grave only in a shroud. Their idyll falls apart when an army officer orders that a Soviet hero, to receive proper honors, must be buried in the prized coffin. Upon the fate of a coffin hangs the fate of private industry: "We are dead men," Arye-Leib despairs, "we are in the hands of Pharoah."

The next crisis to befall these hapless hustlers is compulsory smallpox inoculation. "It won't hurt," the doctor reassures his patient, as have countless physicians before and since, "it doesn't hurt in the soft part." "I have no soft part," the oddly named Meyer Endless replies. True to his heritage, he cannot resist a few choice curses: "Life is a dungheap, the world a whorehouse, and people are crooks." The more reflective Arye-Leib appeals to principle. Once again it is the figure of the mother who stands for life for the sake of life. In homely Yiddish style he argues against submitting

to pain, however beneficent: "Young lady, we were borne by a
mother just as you were. This woman, our mother, bore us that we
should live and not that we should be tortured. She wished that we
should live well, and she was right, as only a mother can be. . . .
Our goal is to live our life to the end, and not torture it, and we
are not fulfilling that goal."

The old folks rebel. Their antagonist, an official in charge of the
cemetery, is one of those rigidly resolute Bolsheviks who fill the
pages of Soviet literature. However, since he is also Jewish, his soul
is tinged with sadness: "Broydin planted his legs . . . wide apart
and listened, not raising his eyes. The brown barricade of his beard
lay motionless on his new jacket; it seemed he was immersed in sad
and peaceful thoughts." The mutiny of these assorted paralytics,
cripples, and the simply senile is a scene of comic hilarity. It is
quickly squelched, and the aged Jews depart their last refuge "along
an unspeakably sorrowful road [that] once led from the cemetery to
Odessa." The story is a swan song for a way of life. Jewish Odessa,
like any community, had its share of fools and sinners. What stuck
in Babel's mind, though, was the creative vitality of its people,
their love of life, and their love of words: "a hundred years of Odessa
history [was] asleep beneath the granite flagstones. He pointed out
the monuments and vaults of the wheat exporters, ships' brokers,
and businessmen who had built the Russian Marseilles where once
had stood the village of Hadjibey. They lay there facing the gates,
Ashkenazis, Hessens, and Efrussis, foppish penny pinchers, philosophical carousers, creators of wealth and of Odessa anecdotes."

"Froim Grach" is dry, almost journalistic, in tone. Submitted
for publication in 1933, it did not appear until the post-Stalin thaw,
in 1964. One can see why: it describes the extermination of Odessa's
gangsters by the state police. Froim, that venerable godfather of
the Jewish mafioso, is slaughtered in Cheka headquarters, where he
has gone to plead for mercy and, incorrigible con-man that he is,
to grease a palm or two. The Chekists are shown to be a cold-
blooded bunch, though there are some differences among them
according to age and geography. An agent from Odessa can feel
respect if not pity for this legendary crook who incarnates so much
of the history of his city and, besides, had fought for the Revolution;
on the other hand, an outsider from Moscow, the Cheka chairman,
takes the whole bloody business quite calmly. A soldier, an older
man, honors the manliness with which Froim died; for a younger

Red Army man "they're all alike"—an enemy of the state is an enemy of the state.

"Arcady" is invoked several times in the story. Several gangsters are ambushed at a spot near the sea called Arcady, and Froim, shortly before his murder, plays with his three-year-old grandson, also named Arcady. "Froim Grach" is an elegy over an idyll. The death of the gangsters, like the expulsion of the aged in "The End of the Old Folk's Home," marks the death of old Odessa—a place which may have been corrupt and poor, but where life was lazy, easy going, and intimate. People knew who you were. The coming of the Chekists—at least its younger and non-Odessan members— means the triumph of an impersonal order. They do not know and do not care to know who Froim is. Froim is not shown in the city itself but on his farm on its outskirts, the lucky inhabitant of a pastoral retreat. When he sets out to meet his death, he walks out of an Eden soon to be lost.

Back to the Civil War

As some late stories revert to the Odessan scene, others go back to the years of Revolution and Civil War. "Doroga" (The road, 1932) is a reworking and elaboration of the earlier "Vecher u imperatritsy" ("Evening at the empress's," 1922). "Ivan-da-Marya" (1932), translated as the "S. S. Cow Wheat," is also of early provenance—Babel dated the manuscript 1920–28. "Staratelnaya zhenshchina" (A hard-working woman, 1928) and "Potseluy" (The kiss, 1937) return to scenes of the Polish campaign. "Sulak" (1937), though it takes place in 1926, has much in common with Babel's war stories.[8]

We may think of roads in terms of their destination or in terms of the traffic—the road to Pittsburgh or the road past our house. In Babel's story "The Road," it goes to St. Petersburg, but that is incidental: his real subject is what it was like to be going anyplace in the year 1918. The young narrator, recently returned from war, is on a train to the capital where a job as translator for the Cheka awaits him:

A telegraph operator . . . entered the car. He stretched out his hand and tapped a finger on his open palm—"Documents on this spot." . . . Next to me slept the school teacher Yehuda Weinberg and his wife. He had married a few days ago and was taking his young bride to St. Petersburg.

The entire trip they had whispered about the integrated teaching method, and then dozed off. They slept, clasping hands, one interlaced with the other.

The telegraph operator read their papers, signed by Lunacharsky, pulled a Mauser with a narrow filthy muzzle from his coat and shot the teacher in the face.

Gratuitous events accumulate, all described in this cool, matter-of-fact manner. Weinberg is killed; the narrator, robbed of his money and clothes, escapes. It is merely a question of luck. Babel organizes his narration so as to underscore the senselessness of the experiences he describes—only after the murder do we learn the attackers are killing Jews, seemingly for the sport of it. The half-frozen narrator makes his way to a hospital where he is treated to a tirade against the Jews; then boards an open railroad car; he and a companion warm each other through the freezing night; in the morning his friend also robs him, and disappears.

The St. Petersburg he arrives at is a city of death: "Nevsky Prospect flowed into the distance like the Milky Way. Horses' corpses lay like roadmarkers. Their legs elevated, the horses supported the falling sky. Their open bellies were clean and glistened." Exhausted, he makes his way to the Anichkov Palace, where the Cheka has set up shop. The combination is bizarre, and so is everything he discovers inside the luxurious palace turned into a Revolutionary command post. The officer he reports to is playing with Emperor Nicholas II's toys; a robe which had once belonged to Alexander III, so enormous he swims in it, is thrown over him; he smokes the czar's cigarettes, each twenty centimeters in length. Imperial Russia appears as Alice's Wonderland, a place where everything was out of proportion and got "curiouser and curiouser."

In this tale of meaningless violence and grotesque incongruities Babel's final two sentences may be the oddest thing of all: "Before a day had passed I had everything—clothes, food, work [translating the depositions of "diplomats, arsonists, and spies"] and comrades, true in friendship and death, comrades of the sort not to be found anyplace in the world, except in our country. Thus thirteen years ago began my excellent life, a life filled with ideas and joy." No doubt Babel was paying Caesar his due. Coming at the end of this particular (and excellent) story, with its grim horrors and bizarre dissonances, the final lines seem to have been written tongue in cheek.

In "Ivan-da-Marya" Babel drew from his experience of 1918 in grain-raising expeditions for the new Revolutionary government. Apparently begun in 1920, its lyricism, violent action, and use of sharp contrasts link it to the *Red Cavalry* cycle. The central contrast is between the German colonists along the Volga, where the ship *Ivan-da-Marya* is lading grain, and the Russians manning the ship. The German and Dutch farms are an island of peace in a sea of war. War is drawing close and no one will escape, but in the interval these industrious and disciplined farmers inhabit an idyll of contentment. The keeper of a local inn is called Biedermeyer, after a style of furniture denoting solid bourgeois comfort. The Russians are a ragtag crew of rejects and drunkards. The ship's captain is a caricature of Russian disorderliness: former tramp, convict, penitent in a monastery, currently a run-down alcoholic. "Mother Russia needs a drink, the Russian soul has finally felt the urge," the Latvian commissar assigned to the ship taunts him, underlining the transparent allegory. Russians drink, but they sing too. Their art shows the same fatality as their personalities: "The strength of Seletsky's voice was quite unnatural. . . . his voice, spreading out limitless and fatal, filled the soul with the sweetness of self-destruction and gypsy oblivion." Captain Korostelyov takes the ship and its drunken crew on a wild night cruise along the Volga in search of moonshine, and rams the vessel into a landing dock on their return. Then another breed of Russians greets him—tough Red Army men from the command of Vasily Chapaev, a legendary hero of the Civil War. They riddle the hapless captain with bullets and arrest the crew. The official in charge of the expedition pronounces the captain's epitaph: "It's all very well to be a fine fellow three times over, to have spent time in hermitages, to have sailed the White Sea, to be generally a desperado; but please don't waste fuel. . . ." If this is the voice of the new Russia, it is almost enough to make one miss the old.

"A Hard-Working Woman" is a reprise of "With Old Man Makhno,"[9] except that the woman with whom Makhno's men take their turn is now a prostitute rather than a victim of rape. It ends sentimentally, with the lonely narrator whispering the woman's poetic name, Anelya, in the dark night.

More interesting is "The Kiss," which brings back Lyutov, as protagonist as well as observer. It is his love story, his kiss. He is billeted in the home of a paralyzed old man, his widowed daughter (her husband was killed in the war against the Germans), and her five-year-old son. A Cossack pal assures him that, though the widow behaves correctly, she is an easy mark. Concerned neighbors descend on the house to protect the widow's virtue, but Lyutov assures her that he is not that sort: "For your information I ought to inform you that I have a law degree, and belong to the so-called class of cultured people."

They become fast friends. Lyutov tells her and her fearful family of the Revolution and its promises, for in those heady days "the future seemed ours for the asking, the war seemed a stormy prologue to happiness, and happiness part of our natures." They kiss, war breaks in, and they separate. Upon his return, Lyutov discovers that the fighting has destroyed her village and left her desolate, and he can do nothing to help. Much of this fine story is told in the factual, documentary manner Babel employed in the thirties, and the last sentence reads like a newspaper report: "A few hours later our brigade passed the old frontier of the Kingdom of Poland." That sentence encapsulates the painful irony of the story. While men and women dream of happiness, history marches along its own path, oblivious of their hopes. Babel had not lost the knack of gaining moving effects through the simplest of means.

"Sulak" recalls the more brutal moments of *Red Cavalry*. A stark tale stripped of authorial comment, it recounts the tracking down by two men, presumably political police agents, of a fugitive Ukrainian nationalist named Sulak. They find him, and one of them shoots him. The other, the narrator, is, like Lyutov, a silent witness of the world's brutality. The story makes us aware of the extent to which the power of *Red Cavalry* is cumulative. "Sulak" is as well done as several pieces in that book but standing alone it is thin and easily forgotten.

Two Paris Stories

"Ulitsa Dante" (Dante Street, 1934) and "Sud" (The trial, 1938) are products of one of Babel's trips to Paris, probably that of 1932–33. He loved Paris but could not bring himself to emigrate ("The Trial" suggests why). Paris in a way recalled the Odessa of his youth, where people simply lived, while in the Soviet Union life lay in the future. As that future was taking shape, men and women argued, fought, murdered each other, struggled and suffered. Russia was tiresome and frightening, but it was also the battleground of history. Paris was a holiday.

"Dante Street" pays tribute to the city, though not without irony. Babel may have had his beloved Maupassant in mind as he wrote it: it is "manufactured" in a way Maupassant's work is often, and Babel's seldom. It is also charming. The French enjoy the refinements of civilization: good food, good literature, and good women. Sex is, like everything else in Paris, a cultivated art. An automobile salesman and neighbor at the Hôtel Danton offers to initiate his Russian friend into the intricacies of French culture. The Russian listens attentively as his mentor makes love to a salesgirl named Germaine in the adjacent room on an appointed schedule. On Sundays and Wednesdays at 5:00 P.M. "their room would resound with growls, the thud of falling bodies, cries of fright, and then the woman's tender death agony would commence: 'Oh, Jean!' " The entire establishment, indeed, seems to be engaged in such systematic passions: "From five to ten the groans of love used to send our hotel, the Hôtel Danton, soaring through the air. Experts were at work in the bedrooms. . . ."

Sadly, Jean is not up to the demands of love. He cheats on Germaine. He is too much the bourgeois auto salesman who wants an orderly life. Germaine plays the game, squeezing herself into a tailored English suit to wait dutifully on customers in a fashionable glove shop on the rue Royale. At heart, however, she is all passion: "Cette femme est folle," Jean complains. "The simple fact that on earth there is winter and summer, beginning and end, that after winter comes summer and contrariwise—all this does not concern Mademoiselle Germaine. Such things are not for her." When she has become too much for Jean to handle and he betrays her, she murders him by slitting his throat from ear to ear. A crowd pours into the corridors of the busy Hôtel Danton—prostitutes, their customers, assorted lovers, curious onlookers. In a babble of voices, some French, others Italian, they deliver their verdict and the moral of the tale: "Dio cartiga quelli, chi non conoseono l'amore"—God punishes those who do not understand love.

"The Trial" is a spare piece—Babel subtitled it "From My Notebook"—but within its limits effective. It describes the melancholy

fate of a Russian émigré, a former nobleman and lieutenant colonel
in the White Army, without letting him speak once. We obtain
most of the information from court proceedings. Nedachin is on
trial for absconding with the valuables of a Madam Blanchard, whom
he had seduced. His life in emigration has been one of aimless
knocking about: work as a policeman in Zagreb, in Paris failure to
pass the test for a taxi driver's license; finally, resorting to hood-
winking lonely old women. By causing the activity of the story to
whirl about this passive, silent figure, Babel underscores his total
alienation: "The speech of others showered on Nedachin like a summer's rain. Helpless, huge, arms dangling, he towered above the
crowd like a sad beast from another world." The documentary presentation and the subtitle suggest that Babel recorded an actual
trial.[10]

"My First Fee"

"Moy pervy gonorar" (My first fee) was dated by Babel 1922–
28, but it never appeared in his lifetime, no doubt because of the
prudishness of Soviet publishers and censors. It is a lovely piece in
which Babel once again goes back to the days of his youth: its
subject is the aches of young desire, the comic awkwardness of early
sexual adventure, the contented glow of sexual satisfaction. "To live
in Tiflis in the springtime, to be twenty years old and not to be
loved is a terrible thing," he begins, in a line he repeats after
demonstrating why indeed it is a terrible thing to be young in Tiflis
and not loved.

Babel is a master of what we might call ironic overstatement, of
hyperboles that succeed beautifully in charming us. His neighbors,
he writes, "crazed with love, turned and twisted like two large fish
in a small tank. The tails of these two frantic fish thrashed against
the wall. They made the whole attic shake—it was burnt black by
the sun—tore it from its foundations and bore it off into infinity.
Their teeth were clenched tight in the relentless fury of their passion.
In the morning the wife, Miliet, went downstairs for bread. She
was so weak she had to hold on to the bannister in order not to
fall."

The young man of the story is a dreamer with little experience
and an aspiring writer with large ambitions. "I thought it was a
waste of time not to write as well as Leo Tolstoy," he recalls. "My

stories were intended to escape oblivion." A man who lives for future glory "is ashamed to cry in sorrow; he hasn't got the sense to laugh in joy. Being a dreamer, I hadn't mastered the absurd art of happiness."

Babel's entire corpus says much the same thing. Happiness is fullness of being, a state of grace like that enjoyed by natural creatures. To the unhappy, happiness must always appear "absurd," for it is beyond the grasp of intention. Benya Krik, Galina Rubtsova of "First Love," many of the Cossacks are "happy," luxuriating in the fullness of the now. To be happy is simply to be. Tied to the tail of his father's ambitions, Babel always spied happiness in the other, in people different from himself: carefree Jewish gangsters, anarchic Cossacks, voluptuous and uninhibited Gentile women.

The happy groans of his neighbors drive him to seek out a prostitute. He suffers the disillusionment of young love: "A large woman with drooping shoulders and a crumpled stomach stood before me. . . . Oh gods of my youth! How different it was, this dreary business, from the love of my neighbors on the other side of the wall, their long, drawn-out squeals." Either to escape her or to win her pity, the young man uses his overcharged imagination to concoct a cock-and-bull story in which he appears as an exploited homosexual prostitute! The woman recognizes a colleague, though of the other sex, and is touched by pity. They tumble into bed, the (female) prostitute whispering gently, "Sister. My little sister," and that night she teaches her co-worker all the tricks of the trade. He takes the next day off from work, and together they indulge in the delight of merely being alive: "The world was beautiful just to give us pleasure." When he offers to pay her, she refuses. The money he thus saves is his "first fee"—for the fanciful yarn he spun for her. It is also, Babel writes, looking back on his life, the largest fee he ever received—because it came not from the cash registers of commerce but "from the hands of love."[11]

An Unfinished Novel: "The Jewess"

Of the several novels Babel is reported to have considered writing—one on the Cheka, another ("Kolya Topuz") on the rehabilitation of a renegade from Soviet society—the only surviving manuscript that seems clearly to be the beginning of a novel is "Evreyka" (The Jewess), which has been dated to 1934. "Gapa

Guzhva" and "Kolyvushka," which some scholars believe are also
parts of a projected novel, do not show a developing plot and may
just as well have been intended for another cycle of stories. In "The
Jewess," on the other hand, Babel appears to be laying the foundation for a full-length novel. It is among the very few of his fictional
writings to employ an omniscient third-person narrator. Characters
are introduced, their histories given, and a situation outlined. The
prose, stripped of Babel's characteristic ornamentalism, is descrip-
tive and detailed, and moves at a leisurely pace, suggesting Babel
felt he had scope to work out his ideas. It is of course difficult to
judge from fragments how a novel might have turned out. Short
stories are like sprints, novels like marathons—in the former you
must do it all at once; in the latter it is the long haul that counts.
Nevertheless, Babel's start is not very promising.

For one thing, Babel was constitutionally incapable of working
with the standard plots of socialist realism. Socialist realism looks
to the future: the past is to be discarded or overcome. Even in these
drearily orthodox pages Babel remains obsessed with that central
issue of the previous decade, the relation of the old and the new
cultures. The old—represented by a *shtetl* or village in the former
Jewish Pale of Settlement—is dying. A young Red Army commissar, Boris Erlich, with a biography quite similar to his creator's,
returns home upon his father's death. He finds a decaying, impoverished community with an aging population waiting to die also.
Though he acknowledges the bond of Jewishness and mortality that
ties him to these unfortunates, Boris knows that the *shtetl's* days are
numbered. Over the course of some maudlin pages, he persuades
his mother to move to Moscow with him, for Moscow is *life*—
activity, thought, the pulse of a brave new world in the making.

In Moscow Boris meets his closest friend Alyosha Selivanov, a
comrade from his days in Budyonny's First Cavalry Army. They
enroll at the War Academy, and set up a commune in Boris's
apartment to study new cavalry tactics. Boris's mother serves these
"Red Marshals," as they are called, Jewish "gefilte fish" and tea.
In her culinary masterpieces "one felt the essence of the Jewish
people, its wholehearted and vehement passion." Boris, we are told,
is deeply committed to his army group, "perhaps because his people
had for so long been denied one of the finest of human feelings—
that of comradeship in the field and in battle. . . ." A wedding
of two cultures occurs as hard-riding Cossack chums munch away

at good old Jewish gefilte fish. Had Babel intended this as a joke he might have gotten a laugh. As it stands, it is little wonder and a great relief that he abandoned it.[12]

Chapter Eleven
Conclusion

Writers do not write to advance literary history. They write because they have something to say or because they want to make something. A great writer may find few followers, whereas a lesser talent, if he hits upon innovations that meet the needs of his age, may have large repercussions. We may turn to literature to discover how men and women in other places and times thought, felt, and lived, but we also read the works of the past for what they may have to say to us.

From the view of literary history Babel comes at the end of an era, though he and his generation did not view themselves so. He lived at a time of revolutionary change when people saw themselves creating the world anew. His own work, like the mass of writing of the 1920s, turns on the anxieties and hopes aroused by an age when the old society was crumbling and an inchoate order was taking shape. But literary history, though linked to political and social history, has its own rhythms. In the history of Russian literature the year 1910 figures larger than 1917, at least in the short run. In the twenties mainstream writers, no matter how they viewed the Revolution in society, were part of a revolution in the arts. That revolution, which began with the prewar reaction against symbolism, was (like all revolutions) only partial. Even as they rejected symbolist metaphysics, the innovative groups—futurists, acmeists, imaginists, ornamentalists—furthered symbolist experimentation in form. Both symbolists and their avant-garde antagonists were united in their rejection of imitative theories of art, whose hegemony had extended from the Greeks through the realism of the nineteenth century. In their attack upon mimetic explanations of art they were heirs of romanticism. For romantics, symbolists, and modernists art is no longer, as it had been for two thousand years, a mirror reflecting reality. It is instead the result of a creative process, whether of mysterious inspiration or laborious craft, that brings something *new* into the world.

146

The abandonment of ideology had consequences that distinguished the modernists from their symbolist predecessors, as much as they owed to them. First, the realist confidence in a common, knowable reality had been shattered; now art's roots in a presumably transcendental reality were severed. The work stood alone, without ties to a sustaining order. Artists focused on the thing itself, its formal patterns. The work became increasingly self-conscious, often self-reflexive, playing upon an ironic skepticism about its relations to the world and to its creator. Everything seemed to converge in paradox. The new became a value in itself, and not for the sake of fashion—the notorious difficulty of the modernists expressed their contempt for the merely voguish—but because tradition was no longer capable of dictating the artist's activity. It was against this background that Babel's highly sophisticated stories were written. Besides their severe formal excellence, the best of them exhibit a penetrating intellectual irony, which holds the pathos of life at a distance, and a preference for ambiguity over unequivocal statement that are hallmarks of the modern.

The Soviet Union has not been a hospitable place for artistic experimentation. In the mid-twenties the radically innovative activity of the avant-garde ceased; with the institution of socialist realism in the thirties, experimentation became the crime of "formalism." The manufacture of art objects became a standardized process, like that of a machine spitting out words or painting by the numbers. It is difficult and perhaps idle to speculate how Russian literature might have developed had its course not been determined by force. The twenties, however, were the high-water mark of modernism, not only in Russia, but in Western Europe and the United States as well. Most of its classic texts are a product of that extraordinary decade in the annals of human creativity: Marcel Proust's *Remembrance of Things Past* (1913–27), Thomas Mann's *The Magic Mountain* (1922), James Joyce's *Ulysses* (1922), T. S. Eliot's *The Waste Land* (1922), Franz Kafka's *The Trial* (1925), *The Castle* (1926), and *Amerika* (1927), Ernest Hemingway's *In Our Time* (1924) and *The Sun Also Rises* (1926), William Faulkner's *The Sound and the Fury* (1929).[1] Modernism in the arts has continued down to our day, but not as the sustained and powerful movement it was in the first third of the century. In the thirties economic depression, the advent of totalitarianism, and the threat of global war compelled writers in the West to address political questions and the problems of contemporary society. As in the Soviet Union, realism reemerged, though the western and Soviet understanding of realism have little in common. As early as 1931 Edmund Wilson in his pioneering study *Axel's Castle* announced of such modernists as Eliot, Proust, Yeats, and Joyce that "though we shall continue to admire them as masters, [they] will no longer serve us as guides."[2]

With the relative relaxation of controls in the post-Stalin years, artists in the Soviet Union have sought to rediscover a personal idiom. Writers once again write of love, nature, personal and family problems, often with great sensitivity, but with a few exceptions literature remains conservative in its expressive means. Solzhenitsyn's views, in the Soviet context, are radical, but formally his novels are a throwback to nineteenth-century fiction. Russia, not so long ago in the vanguard of the arts, has become a provincial backwater, and the situation is not helped by the continual emigration, sometimes by expulsion, of the more venturesome of Soviet artists. Babel is read, but not imitated. Soviet writers are more likely to follow the example of Chekhov than the modernists of our century. Just as the daring style of his work places Babel in the heroic age of modernism, so the subject matter with which he is most identified, the Civil War, places him in the heroic age of the Russian Revolution. As Soviet society has stabilized, writers have turned their attention from events of cataclysmic drama to the nuances of daily life. Ambitions have become more modest, expressive means more restrained. Moreover, there are writers who, no matter what the requirements of the age, are dangerous to follow, and Babel may be one of them. His voice, a rich and startling compound of lyricism, pathos, mystery, comedy, and irony, is so individual that it is difficult to conceive of anyone else sounding like him.

But we do not judge writers by their influence. We want them to have written well. Babel meets that test as well as any Russian writer of prose fiction in our century. Literature is one of the activities by which people make sense of their experience. For Russians, Babel and the other courageously honest writers of the twenties provide access to their own tormented history. There is no subject more closed to debate in the Soviet Union than the Revolution. If the doors are ever opened to free discussion, Babel's work will be a major source for a criticism unafraid to explore the meanings of that momentous event. Revolution is change, and we are all in this century of rapid transformation of our planet the children of revolution. Babel is a writer of crisis (hence his high-pitched voice). His fiction gives us a sense of what it is like to be alive when the mainstays of traditional culture have disintegrated and the shape of the future is an open question.

Notes and References

There is no complete edition of Babel's works. They are cited here, unless noted otherwise, according to I. Babel', *Izbrannoe* (Moscow, 1966)— quotations in the text are abbreviated as *I* followed by page number. Since many of Babel's stories are extremely short, making location of citations easy, reference to pages are usually omitted when the title of the work is given in the text. Original sources of publication are provided only for works not in *Izbrannoe,* where details of publication may be found in the notes. Though transliteration in the text is in a popular form, citations in Notes and References and the Bibliography are according to the Library of Congress system. I have made use of the excellent translations in Isaac Babel, *The Collected Stories,* ed. and trans. Walter Morison (New York, 1955), but I have often modified them.

Preface

1. Iurii Tynianov, *Arkhaisty i novatory* (Leningrad: Priboi, 1929), 15.

Chapter One

1. Judith Stora-Sandor, *Isaac Babel': l'homme et l'oeuvre* (Isaac Babel: The man and his work) (Paris, 1968), 18.
2. For a more detailed geography, see Salo W. Baron, *The Russian Jew Under the Tsars and Soviets* (New York: Macmillan, 1964), 39.
3. Cited in S. M. Dubnow, *History of the Jews in Russia and Poland,* trans. I. Friedlander, 3 vols. (Philadelphia: Jewish Publication Society, 1916–20), 2:191. The notorious "Pobedonostsev formula" for the solution of the Jewish problem was: "One-third will die out, one-third will leave the country, and one-third will be completely dissolved in the surrounding population" (ibid., 3:10). (Konstantin Pobedonostsev, procurator of the Holy Synod, wielded enormous power in the reigns of Alexander III and Nicholas II.)
4. Baron, *Russian Jew,* 114.
5. Cited in Dubnow, *History of the Jews,* 2:55.
6. Cited in Lucy S. Dawidowicz, ed., *The Golden Tradition: Jewish Life and Thought in Eastern Europe* (New York: Holt, Rinehart & Winston, 1967), 161.
7. See Louis Greenberg, *The Jews in Russia,* 2 vols. (New Haven: Yale University Press, 1944–51), 2:57–58.

8. See the reminiscences of Babel's sister, in Stora-Sandor, *Isaac Babel'*, 19–20.

9. O. Mandel'shtam, *Shum vremeni* (The noise of time) (Leningrad: Vremia, 1925), 17.

10. See *Isaac Babel: The Lonely Years 1925–1939*, ed. Nathalie Babel (New York, 1964), 302, 366; my italics.

11. Stanza 20 from "Fragments of Onegin's Journey," in *Eugene Onegin: A Novel in Verse by Aleksandr Pushkin*, trans. Vladimir Nabokov, Bollingen Series, no. 72 (New York: Pantheon, 1964), 1:340.

12. "Odessa," in *Konarmiia; Odesskie rasskazy; P'esy* (Red cavalry; Odessa tales; plays) (Chicago, 1965), 155–58.

13. Ibid.

14. Ibid.

15. Ibid. The Maupassant story Babel refers to is "L'Aveu" (The avowal).

16. *Lonely Years*, xiv–xv.

17. Ibid., xvi.

18. Memoirs of Sergei Bondarin and S. Gekht in *I. Babel': Vospominaniia sovremennikov* (Babel: Memoirs by contemporaries), ed. A. Pirozhkova and N. Iurgeneva (Moscow, 1972), 133, 67–68; *Lonely Years*, xvi. See also U. Spektor, "Molodoi Babel' " (The young Babel), *Voprosy literatury* (Problems of literature), no. 7 (1982):278–81, which corrects many of the factual errors that have crept into Babel's biographies and also gives his sister's recollections.

19. See the memoir of Il'ia Erenburg, in *Vospominaniia*, 50–64.

20. *Lonely Years*, 146; *Izbrannoe*, 259.

21. *Lonely Years*, 87.

22. Ibid., 160, 348.

23. Ibid., 138. See 143: "Worrying about you people [his mother and sister] has made me itch all over. Apparently traits inherited from my mother's side are beginning to make themselves felt."

24. Cited by A. N. Pirozhkova, in *Vospominaniia*, 345.

25. *Lonely Years*, 191, 154.

26. Cited by G. Munblit, in *Vospominaniia*, 129.

27. *Lonely Years*, 135.

28. Ibid., 278.

29. In Stora-Sandor, *Isaac Babel'*, 16.

30. "Avtobiografiia" (Autobiography), in *Izbrannoe*, 23. The stories have not survived.

31. *Lonely Years*, xvii.

32. Ibid.

33. Cited by Nadezhda Mandelstam, in *Hope Against Hope: A Memoir*, trans. Max Hayward (New York, 1976), 321.

34. "Nachalo," in *Izbrannoe*, 315–18.

35. Nathalie Babel disputes this, in *Lonely Years*, xiv. The source is Babel himself, in "Avtobiografiia," in *Izbrannoe*, 24.

36. The diary is quoted extensively and excerpted in *Literaturnoe nasledstvo* (Literary heritage) 74 (1965):474–82, 490–99.

37. For details of publication, see *Izbrannoe*, 462–67.

38. Konstantin Paustovsky, *Years of Hope: The Story of a Life*, trans. Manya Harari and Andrew Thomson (New York, 1968), 121; Konstantin Fedin, *Gorkii sredi nas* (Gorky among us) (Moscow: Molodaia gvardiia, 1967), 216.

39. S. Budennyi, "Babizm Babelia iz *Krasnoi novi*" (Babel as an old woman in *Red Virgin Soil*), *Oktiabr'* (October), no. 3 (1924):196–97. The *Pravda* article and a summary of the debate are in *Literaturnoe nasledstvo* (Literary heritage) 74:500–505. Budyonny's open letter of 1928 and Gorky's reply are in *Lonely Years*, 384–89. Stalin is quoted by Ervin Sinkó, *Roman eines Romans: Moskauer Tagebuch* (The romance of a novel: Moscow diary) (Cologne, 1962), 315.

40. *Lonely Years*, 61.

41. S. Grigor'ev, in *Literaturnoe nasledstvo* (Literary heritage) 70 (1963):134.

42. See H. G. Scott, ed., *Problems of Soviet Literature: Reports and Speeches at the First Writers' Congress* (1935; reprint ed., Westport, Conn.: Hyperion, 1981), 15–24.

43. Cited by Sinkó, *Roman eines Romans*, 314.

44. Gekht, in *Vospominaniia*, 72.

45. See *Lonely Years*, xxi; Iurii Annenkov, *Dnevnik moikh vstrech* (Diary of my encounters) (New York, 1966), 1:306. Ilya Ehrenburg says that Babel was more aware than most of the realities of the purges. See *Men, Years—Life*, vol. 4, *Eve of War: 1933–41*, trans. Tatiana Shebunina and Yvonne Kapp (London, 1963), 197.

46. *Znamia* (Banner), no. 8 (1964):149–50; *Izbrannoe*, 442; *Lonely Years*, 281, 264, 189.

47. See Robert Conquest, *The Great Terror: Stalin's Purge of the Thirties* (London: Macmillan, 1968), 467, 322.

48. *Lonely Years*, xxvi–xxvii.

Chapter Two

1. Alexander Blok, "Krushenie gumanizma" (The collapse of humanism), in *Sobranie sochinenii* (Collected works), 6 vols. (Leningrad: Khud. lit., 1982), 4:334–40.

2. Andrei Belyi, "Magiia slov" (The magic of words), in *Simvolizm* (Symbolism) (Moscow: Musaget, 1910), 431; J. Holthusen, *Studien zur Ästhetik und Poetik des russischen Symbolismus* (Studies in the aesthetics and

poetics of Russian symbolism) (Göttingen: Vandenhoeck & Ruprecht, 1957), 32.

3. Nikolai Gumilev, "Nasledie simvolizma i akmeizm" (The inheritance of symbolism and acmeism), *Apollon* (Apollo) 4, no. 1 (1913):43; D. Chizhevskii, "O poezii russkogo futurizma" (On the poetry of Russian futurism), *Novyi zhurnal* (New review) 73 (1963):141–42.

4. See Milton Ehre, "Zamjatin's Aesthetics," *Slavic and East European Journal* 19, no. 3 (Fall 1975):288–96.

5. Cited by Konstantin Paustovsky, "Reminiscences of Babel," in *Dissonant Voices in Soviet Literature,* ed. Patricia Blake & Max Hayward (New York, 1964), 46–51.

6. James E. Falen, *Isaac Babel: Russian Master of the Short Story* (Knoxville, Tenn., 1974), 13.

7. *Dissonant Voices,* 46–48.

8. *Nash sovremennik* (Our contemporary), no. 4 (1964):98–99.

Chapter Three

1. *Ogni* (Lights), no. 6 (1913):3–4. In English, in Isaac Babel, *The Forgotten Prose,* ed. and trans. Nicholas Stroud (Ann Arbor, 1978), 17–21.

2. *Literaturnoe nasledstvo* (Literary heritage) 74:483–88. Another early story on a Jewish theme is described on 471–72. For an English translation of "Childhood at Grandmother's," see Isaac Babel, *You Must Know Everything: Stories 1915–37* (New York, 1966), 5–12.

3. *Letopis'* (Chronicle), no. 11 (1916):32–44; reprinted in *Znamia* (Banner), no. 8 (1964):126–31 and *Izbrannoe,* 191–94; *The Lonely Years,* 38–52.

4. *Zhurnal zhurnalov* (Journal of journals), no. 48 (1916):11–12; no. 49 (1916):7; no. 51 (1916):4–5; no. 7 (1917):8–9; no. 16 (1917):11. "Publichnaia biblioteka" and "Deviat' " have been reprinted in *Novoe russkoe slovo* (New Russian word), 29 March 1964; "Vdokhnovenie," in *Znamia* (Banner), no. 8 (1964):122–24; for "Odessa," see above, chap. 1, n. 12. In English, in *You Must Know,* 13–34. On 21 March 1918 Babel published a second sketch of Odessa in *Vechernaia zvezda* (Evening star).

5. *Svobodnye mysli* (Free thoughts), 13 March 1917; reprinted in *Nash sovremennik* (Our contemporary), no. 10 (1965):65–67; *Forgotten Prose,* 26–28.

6. For a bibliography of the *Novaia zhizn'* (New life) sketches, see Danuta Mendelson, *Metaphor in Babel's Short Stories* (Ann Arbor, 1982), 139. They have been reprinted in Yugoslavia, in *Zbornik za Slavistiku* (Slavic miscellany), no. 1 (1970):113–35. In English, in *Forgotten Prose,* 29–84, and *You Must Know,* 47–74. Most of them appeared under the heading, *Dnevnik* (Diary); two of the *Diary* pieces published in *Forgotten*

Prose, "Na dvortsovoi ploshchadi" (On palace square) and "Kontsert v Katerinenshtadte" (A concert in Katerinenstadt) appeared in *Zhizn' iskusstva* (Life of art), 11 and 13 November 1918; reprinted in *Zvezda* (Star), no. 11 (1967):227–29.

7. Cited from *Forgotten Prose,* 60; *You Must Know,* 65–66, 55–56.

8. *Novaia zhizn'* (New life), 28 May 1918.

9. It was subtitled "Iz tsikla Gershele" (From the cycle *Hershele*), but Babel did not add to it.

10. Originally in *Lava,* no. 1 (June 1920):10–13; "Na pole chesti" has been republished in *Vozdushnie puti* (Aerial ways) 3 (1963):52–53; "Dezertir," "Semeistvo papashi Maresko," and "Kvaker" in *Filologicheskii sbornik* (Philological miscellany) (Alma Ata), nos. 8–9:199–202; all four, in English, in *You Must Know,* 75–94; Gaston Vidal, *Figures et anecdotes de la Grande Guerre* (People and tales from the Great War) (Paris: La Renaissance du Livre, 1918).

11. *You Must Know,* 78–79, 86.

12. See *Literaturnoe nasledstvo* (Literary heritage) 74:488; *Znamia* (Banner), no. 6 (1972):214–15; *Voprosy literatury* (Problems of literature), no. 4 (1979):160–63.

13. See *Forgotten Prose,* 81–109.

14. Originally in *Siluety* (Silhouettes), no. 1 (1922):7, under the heading "Iz peterburgskogo dnevnika" (From a Petersburg diary); republished in *Znamia* (Banner), no. 8 (1964):135–37; in English, in *You Must Know,* 95–102.

Chapter Four

1. An additional Odessa story was discovered in 1974, "Spravedlivost' v skobkakh" (Justice in brackets, 1921), in *Prostor* (Expanse), no. 1 (1974):79–81. It is inferior to the others. Stories referred to in this chapter and chapters 6, 7, and 9 are all from *Izbrannoe.*

2. See Maurice Samuel, *The World of Sholom Aleichem* (New York: Knopf, 1944), 212.

3. Robert Alter, *Defenses of the Imagination: Jewish Writers and Modern Historical Crisis* (Philadelphia: Jewish Publication Society of America, 1977), 156.

Chapter Five

1. Originally in *Siluety* (Silhouettes), nos. 8–9 (1923):5–6; republished in *Krasnaia nov'* (Red virgin soil), no. 4 (1924):9–11; in English, in *Lonely Years,* 53–56.

2. *Siluety* (Silhouettes), no. 12 (1923):5–6; *Krasnaia nov'* (Red virgin soil), no. 4 (1924):11–12; *You Must Know,* 115–17.

3. *Krasnaia nov'* (Red virgin soil), no. 4 (1924):12–13; *Collected Stories*, 278–80. Makhno was a Ukrainian anarchist.

4. Originally in *Izvestiia* (News) (Odessa), 23 February 1923; republished in *Zvezda vostoka* (Star of the East), no. 3 (1967); in English, in *You Must Know*, 123–24 (the diary entries are given on 122).

5. *Novyi zhurnal* (New review), no. 5 (June 1969):16–20; in English, as "And Then There Were None," in *You Must Know*, 129–33.

6. *Literaturnaia Rossiia* (Literary Russia), no. 47 (24 November 1964); *You Must Know*, 141–54.

7. *Siluety* (Silhouettes), nos. 6–7 (1923):5; *Pereval* (The pass), no. 6 (1928); in English, as "The Chinaman," in *You Must Know*, 107–9. The subtitle suggests Babel had a cycle in mind.

8. *Siluety* (Silhouettes), no. 12 (1923):5; *Pereval* (The pass), no. 6 (1928); *Collected Stories*, 363–65.

Chapter Six

1. *Voprosy literatury* (Problems of literature), no. 4 (1964):120.

2. "Babel saw Russia," writes Viktor Shklovskii, "as a French writer attached to Napoleon's army might have seen her" ("I. Babel': kriticheskii romans" [Babel: A critical romance], *LEF*, no. 2 [1924]:154).

3. See A. Voronskii, *Literaturno-kriticheskie stat'i* (Critical articles) (Moscow, 1963), 289–90.

4. Renato Poggioli, "Isaak Babel in Retrospect," in *The Phoenix and the Spider* (Cambridge, Mass., 1957), 235.

5. Albert Cook speaks of "the simple declarative base" of epic and of "the relation between statement and rhythm [that] is one of contrast or counterpoint" (*The Classic Line: A Study in Epic Poetry* [Bloomington: Indiana University Press, 1966], 11).

6. Babel habitually spoke of his language in military terms: style is an "army of words . . . in which all kinds of weapons come into play. No iron can enter the human heart so chillingly as a period put at the right place" (*Izbrannoe*, 273); "A short story must have the precision of a military communique. . . . It must be written in the same firm, straightforward hand one uses for commands . . ." (*Dissonant Voices*, ed. Blake and Hayward, 34–35).

7. See Victor Terras, "Line and Color: The Structure of I. Babel's Short Stories in *Red Cavalry*," *Studies in Short Fiction* 3 (Winter 1966):141–56.

8. Shklovskii, "I. Babel'," 154.

9. Aristotle, *Politics* 1.2.1253a.

10. "Argamak" was not part of the original edition, but was added to the fifth and sixth edition of 1931. Had "The Rabbi's Son" concluded

the work, Lyutov would have been left in a state of mourning; as we have *Red Cavalry* now he moves past grief to the threshold of action.
    11. See Robert A. Maguire, *Red Virgin Soil: Soviet Literature in the 1920's* (Princeton, 1968), 328–29.

Chapter Seven

    1. See above, chap. 2.
    2. The reference to the Talmud ("Oh the rotted Talmuds of my childhood") has been expurgated from more recent Soviet editions. See *Konarmiia* (Moscow, 1926), 35.
    3. Maurice Samuel, *The World of Sholom Aleichem* (New York, 1944), 193–96.

Chapter Eight

    1. Babel's two plays are in *Izbrannoe*. The story "Zakat" (1925) probably served as a basis for the play. See above, chap. 5.
    2. "Otets," in *Izbrannoe*, 179.
    3. *Lonely Years*, 232.
    4. *Benia Krik: Kinopovest'* (Moscow: Krug, 1926).
    5. *Bluzhdaiushchie zvezdy: Kinostsenarii* (Wandering stars: filmscript) (Moscow: Kinopechat, 1926).
    6. Katerina Clark quotes an engineer who, after meeting with Stalin, reported: "For Stalin there are no limits, no canons, and no traditions that he will not break" (*The Soviet Novel: History of a Ritual* [Chicago: University of Chicago Press, 1981], 141).
    7. In *Iskusstvo kino* (Art of the film), no. 5 (1963):57–78. It has not been turned into a film. A section of a film scenario of Nikolai Ostrovskii's novel *How the Steel Was Tempered* was published in *Literaturnaia gazeta* (Literary gazette), 30 October 1938. "Kitaiskaia mel'nitsa" (The Chinese mill), which was filmed in 1928, and "Probnaia mobilizatsiia" (A trial mobilization) have been published in *Ulbandus Review* 1, no. 2 (Spring 1978):86–156.

Chapter Nine

    1. The ending, because of the reference to Trotsky, has been cut from Soviet editions.
    2. The view was central to the critical school of Russian formalism, especially Viktor Shklovsky.

Chapter Ten

    1. Cited from Gleb Struve, *Russian Literature Under Lenin and Stalin* (Norman, Okla., 1971), 262. For the full text, see Scott, ed., *Problems of Soviet Literature*, 13–24.

2. In these years he published one story, "Staratel'naia zhenshchina" (A hard-working woman, 1928), the play *Zakat* (Sunset, 1928), the film-script *Benia Krik* (1926), a two-page "Avtobiografiia" (Autobiography) in the collection *Pisateli: Avtobiografii i portrety sovremennykh russkikh prozaikov* (Autobiographies and portraits of contemporary Russian prose writers), ed. V. Lidin (Moscow: Sovremennye problemy, 1926), and a chapter, "Na birzhu truda" (To the employment office), of a collective novel (by 25 writers!), in *Ogonek* (Light), no. 9 (1927):8–9.

3. *Nash sovremennik* (Our contemporary), no. 4 (1964):97; *Izbrannoe*, 456.

4. *Izbrannoe*, 431, 443, 454–56; *Lonely Years*, 275.

5. See above, chap. 1.

6. "Gapa Guzhva," with the subtitle "The First Chapter of *Velikaia Krinitsa*," in *Novyi mir* (New world), no. 10 (1931):17–20; "Kolyvushka," in *Vozdushnye puti* (Aerial ways) 3 (1963):45–51. Both stories in English, in *Lonely Years*, 3–9, 30–37. Another story from this cycle, "Adrian Morinets," was announced in *Novyi mir* but has never appeared.

7. It was dated by Babel 1920–29.

8. "Ivan-da-Mar'ia," in *30 dnei* (30 days), no. 4 (1932):13–17; in English as "The S. S. Cow-Wheat," in *Collected Stories*, 314–28. "Staratel'naia zhenshchina," in *Pereval* (The pass), no. 6 (1928):188–90; in English, in *You Must Know*, 155–62. For "Doroga," "Potselui," and "Sulak," see *Izbrannoe*.

9. See above, chap. 5.

10. There is evidence that "Ulitsa Dante" was based on a murder trial Babel attended. See *Izbrannoe*, 470–71.

11. *Vozdushnye puti* (Aerial ways) 3 (1963):35–44; in English, in *Lonely Years*, 21–29.

12. *Novyi zhurnal* (New review), no. 95 (June 1969):5–16; in English, in *You Must Know*, 163–84.

Chapter Eleven

1. A comparison of *Red Cavalry* with Hemingway's *In Our Time*, which it in some way resembles, might be interesting.

2. Edmund Wilson, *Axel's Castle: A Study in the Imaginative Literature of 1870–1930* (New York: Charles Scribner's Sons, 1931), 292.

Selected Bibliography

PRIMARY SOURCES

1. Editions of Babel's Works in Russian
a. Collections
Izbrannoe (Selected works). Moscow: Goslitizdat, 1957.
Izbrannoe (Selected works). Moscow: Khudozhestvennaia literatura, 1966.
Izbrannoe (Selected works). Kemerovo: Kemerovskoe knizhnoe izdatel'stvo, 1966.
Konarmiia; Odesskie rasskazy; P'esy (Red Cavalry; Odessa Tales; Plays). Chicago: Russian Language Specialties; Letchworth, Hertfordshire, England: Bradda, 1965.
"Zabytye rasskazy" (Forgotten stories). *Znamia* (Banner), no. 8 (1964):122–45.
Zabytye rasskazy; Iz pisem k druz'iam (Forgotten stories; Letters to friends). Chicago: Russian Language Specialties; Letchworth, Hertfordshire, England: Bradda, 1965.

b. Major Works
Konarmiia (Red Cavalry). Moscow: Gosizdat, 1926.
Konarmiia (Red Cavalry). 5th and 6th rev. eds. Moscow: Gosizdat, 1931.

c. Miscellaneous
"Iz pisem k druz'iam" (Letters to friends). Edited by L. Livshits. *Znamia* (Banner), no. 8 (1964):146–65.
"Materialy k tvorcheskoi biografii I. Babelia" (Materials for a creative biography of I. Babel). Edited with an introduction by L. Livshits. *Voprosy literatury* (Problems of literature), no. 4 (1964):110–35.
"Novye materialy" (New materials). Edited by A. N. Pirozhkova and with notes by I. A. Smirdin. *Literaturnoe nasledstvo* (Literary heritage), 74:467–512. Moscow: Nauka, 1965.
"Vyderzhki iz pisem I. E. Babelia k materi i sestre" (Excerpts from Babel's letters to his mother and sister). *Vozdushnye puti: Al'manakh* (Aerial ways: Almanac) 3:101–15. New York: R. N. Grynberg, 1963.

2. Translations
Benia Krik: A Film-Novel. Translated by Ivor Montagu and S. S. Nalbandov. London: Collet's, 1935.

159

Benya Krik, the Gangster and Other Stories. Edited by Avrahm Yarmolinsky. New York: Schocken, 1948.

The Collected Stories. Edited and translated by Walter Morison, with an introduction by Lionel Trilling. Cleveland: Criterion, 1955.

The Forgotten Prose. Edited and translated by Nicholas Stroud. Ann Arbor: Ardis, 1978.

Isaac Babel: The Lonely Years 1925–1939. Edited by Nathalie Babel. Translated by Max Hayward and Andrew R. MacAndrew. New York: Farrar, Straus & Giroux, 1964.

Lyubka the Cossack and Other Stories. Translated by Andrew R. MacAndrew. New York: Signet, 1963.

Maria. Translated by Denis Caslon. *Tri-Quarterly* 5 (1966):7–36.

Marya. Translated by Michael Glenny and H. Shukman. In *Three Soviet Plays.* Middlesex, England: Penguin, 1966.

Sunset. Translated by Raymond Rosenthal and Mirra Ginsburg. *Noonday* 3. New York: Noonday, 1960.

You Must Know Everything: Stories 1915–1937. Edited by Nathalie Babel. Translated by Max Hayward. New York: Farrar, Straus & Giroux, 1966.

SECONDARY SOURCES

Annenkov, Iurii. *Dnevnik moikh vstrech* (Diary of my encounters). Vol. 1. New York: Inter-Language Literary Associates, 1966. An important memoir. Annenkov knew Babel in Paris, where he spoke openly of his situation in the Soviet Union.

Brown, Edward J. *Russian Literature Since the Revolution.* Rev. ed. Cambridge, Mass.: Harvard University Press, 1982. An admirably balanced history.

Carden, Patricia. *The Art of Isaac Babel.* Ithaca, N.Y.: Cornell University Press, 1972. A sound and sober study. Well-researched.

Cukierman, Walenty. "The Odessa Myth and Idiom in Some Early Works of Odessa Writers." *Canadian-American Slavic Studies* 14, no. 1 (Spring 1980):36–51. A valuable survey.

Ehre, Milton. "Babel's *Red Cavalry*": Epic and Pathos, History and Culture." *Slavic Review* 40, no. 2 (1981):228–40. A more concise version of the argument presented in chapter 5 of this book.

Erenburg [Ehrenburg], Il'ia. *Liudu, gody, zhizn'* (Men, years, life). In *Sobranie sochinenii* (Collected works). Vols. 8–9. Moscow: Khudozhestvennaia literatura, 1966.

———. *People and Life: 1891–1921.* Translated by Anna Bostock and Yvonne Kapp. New York: Knopf, 1962.

————. *Men, Years—Life*. Vol. 2. *First Years of Revolution: 1918–1921*. Translated by Anna Bostock with Yvonne Kapp; Vol. 3. *Truce: 1921– 1933*. Translated by Tatiana Shebunina with Yvonne Kapp; Vol. 4. *Eve of War: 1933–1944*. Translated by Tatiana Shebunina with Yvonne Kapp. London: MacGibbon & Kee, 1962–63. Ehrenburg, an astute observer, knew Babel over the years. His memoirs are a valuable source on the Soviet scene as well as Babel.

Falen, James E. *Isaac Babel: Russian Master of the Short Story*. Knoxville: University of Tennessee Press, 1974. All in all the best book on Babel. Thoroughly researched, it gives close readings of the texts, often discerning, and places them accurately in the history of Russian literature. Includes a helpful annotated bibliography.

Friedberg, Maurice. "Yiddish Folklore Motifs in Isaac Babel's *Konarmija*." In *American Contributions to the Eighth International Congress of Slavists*, Edited by Victor Terras, 192–203. Columbus: Slavica, 1978. Informative.

Gorbachev, Georgii. "O tvorchestve Babelia i po povodu nego" (On Babel's work and on him). *Zvezda* (Star), no. 4 (1925):270–86. A contemporary reaction by a critic sensitive to Babel's style and the genre of his work in the context of current Russian literature.

Grøngaard, Ragna. *An Investigation of Composition and Theme in Isaak Babel's Literary Cycle "Konarmija."* Aarhus, Denmark: Arkona, 1979. Studious.

Hallet, R. W. *Isaac Babel*. Letchworth, Hertfordshire, England: Bradda, 1972. An introduction to the author and his works.

Holthusen, Johannes. *Russische Gegenwartsliteratur* (Modern Russian literature). Vol. 1. *1890–1940*. Bern: Franke, 1963.

————. *Twentieth-Century Russian Literature*. Translated by Theodore Huebner. New York: F. Ungar, 1972. The work of an exceptionally knowledgeable scholar.

Howe, Irving. "The Genius of Isaac Babel." *New York Review of Books*, 20 August 1964, 14–15. An appraisal by an outstanding critic.

Hyman, Stanley Edgar. "Identities of Isaac Babel." *Hudson Review* 8 (1956):620–27. A probing essay that describes the basic opposition in Babel's works as one of nature and culture.

Kazanskii, B. V. and Tynianov, Iu. N., eds. *I. E. Babel': Stat'i i materialy* (Babel: articles and materials). Mastera sovremennoi literatury (Masters of contemporary literature), vol. 2. Leningrad: Academia, 1928. Includes an excellent article with fine insights into the style of the stories by N. Stepanov, "Novella Babelia" (Babel's short story) and a first-rate piece on the play *Zakat* (Sunset) by G. A. Gukovskii.

Levin, F. *I. Babel'*. Moscow: Khudozhestvennaia literatura, 1972. Helpful material.

Luplow, Carol. *Isaac Babel's "Red Cavalry."* Ann Arbor: Ardis, 1982. A close reading. Frequently sensitive.

Maguire, Robert A. *Red Virgin Soil: Soviet Literature in the 1920's.* Princeton: Princeton University Press, 1968. An excellent, often brilliant book, with some fine pages on Babel.

Mandelstam, Nadezhda. *Hope Against Hope.* Translated by Max Hayward. New York: Atheneum, 1976.

————. *Vospominaniia* (Memoirs). New York: Chekhov, 1970. These great memoirs of the Soviet era include some interesting remarks about Babel.

Marcus, Steven. "The Stories of Isaac Babel." *Partisan Review* 22 (1955):400–411. A sophisticated critic takes Babel to task for his supposed glorification of violence.

Marder, Herbert. "The Revolutionary Art of Isaac Babel." *Novel: A Forum on Fiction,* Fall 1963, 54–61. An intelligent essay that identifies Babel's art with the revolutionary experience.

Mendelsohn, Danuta. *Metaphor in Babel's Short Stories.* Ann Arbor: Ardis, 1982. Includes a helpful bibliography.

Mirsky, D. S. *Contemporary Russian Literature.* New York: Knopf, 1926. Though writing too early to see Babel full, Mirsky displays the same lively intelligence that makes his *A History of Russian Literature* a classic.

Morachevskii, N. Ia., ed. *Russkie sovetskie pisateli: prozaiki, Bibliograficheskii ukazatel'* (Soviet Russian writers: prose writers, a bibliography). Vol. 1. Leningrad: Publichnaia biblioteka, 1959. Includes data on first publications and editions of Babel's works.

Murphy, A. B. "The Style of Isaak Babel'." *The Slavonic and East European Review* 44 (1966):361–80. A competent introduction to the topic.

O'Connor, Frank. "The Romanticism of Violence." In *The Lonely Voice: A Study of the Short Story.* Cleveland: World, 1962. Some incisive comments.

Paustovskii, Konstantin. *Povest' o zhizni* (The story of a life). 2 vols. Moscow: Sovetskaia Rossiia, 1966.

————. "Reminiscences of Babel." In *Dissonant Voices in Soviet Literature.* Edited by Patricia Blake and Max Hayward. New York: Harper & Row, 1964. An abridged version.

————. *Years of Hope (The Story of a Life).* Translated by Manya Harari and Andrew Thomson. New York: Pantheon, 1968. The fullest statement of Babel's views of literature may be found in this important memoir.

Pirozhkova, A. and Iurgeneva, N., eds. *I. Babel': Vospominaniia sovremennikov* (Babel: memoirs by contemporaries). Moscow: Sovetskii pisatel', 1972. An indispensable collection of memoirs of Babel through the twenties and thirties. Includes the recollections of Ehrenburg and Paustovsky abridged.

Poggioli, Renato. "Isaac Babel in Retrospect." In *The Phoenix and the Spider.* Cambridge, Mass.: Harvard University Press, 1957, 229–38. A provocative and illuminating essay describing *Red Cavalry* as structured around the literary modes of epos and pathos.

Pozner, Vladimir. *Panorama de la littérature russe contemporaine* (Panorama of contemporary Russian literature). Paris: Kra, 1929. An insightful contemporary history that should be better known.

Rosenthal, Raymond. "The Fate of Isaak Babel: A Child of the Russian Emancipation." *Commentary,* no. 3 (February 1947):126–31. A sensitive discussion of Babel's dilemma as a Jew.

Rzhevskii, Leonid. "Babel'-stilist" (Babel as a stylist). In *Vozdushnye puti: Al'manakh 3* (Aerial ways: almanac 3). New York: R. N. Grynberg, 1963, 217–41. An excellent study. Includes some convincing comparisons to other Odessa writers.

Shklovskii, V. "I. Babel' (kriticheskii romans)" (Babel [A critical romance]). *LEF* 2, no. 6 (1924):152–55. A brilliantly suggestive piece.

————. "Iugo-zapad" (Southwest). *Literaturnaia gazeta* (Literary gazette), 5 January 1933. A description of the "Odessan" or "Southern School" of Soviet literature.

Sinkó, Ervin. *Roman eines Romans: Moskauer Tagebuch* (The romance of a novel: Moscow diary). Cologne: Wissenschaft & Politik, 1962. Sinkó lived with Babel in 1935–36, and his memoirs are of exceptional value.

Sinyavsky, A. "Isaac Babel." In *Major Soviet Writers.* Edited by Edward J. Brown. London: Oxford University Press, 1973. A competent essay by an outstanding critic.

Slonim, Marc. *Modern Russian Literature: From Chekhov to the Present.* New York: Oxford University Press, 1963. A popular history.

Spektor, U. "Molodoi Babel' " (The young Babel). *Voprosy literatury* (Problems of literature), no. 7 (1982):278–81. On the basis of official documents establishes a chronology of Babel's early years.

Stora-Sandor, Judith. *Isaac Babel': L'Homme et l'oeuvre* (Babel: the man and his work). Paris: Klincksieck, 1968. A solid book. The author's interview of Babel's sister is one of the very few accounts of his childhood other than his own.

Struve, Gleb. *Russian Literature Under Lenin and Stalin: 1917–1953.* Norman: University of Oklahoma Press, 1971. The most comprehensive and detailed of Western histories of Soviet literature.

Terras, Victor. "Line and Color: The Structure of I. Babel's Short Stories in *Red Cavalry.*" *Studies in Short Fiction* 3, no. 2 (1966):141–56. A penetrating discussion of the interplay of epic, dramatic, and lyric elements in *Red Cavalry* and the function of "travesty."

Trilling, Lionel. Introduction to *The Collected Stories,* by Isaac Babel. Cleveland: Criterion, 1955. A very fine interpretive essay.

Van der Eng, J. "La description poétique chez Babel" (Poetic description in Babel). In *Dutch Contributions to the Fifth International Congress of Slavicists.* The Hague: Mouton, 1963. A meticulous though far from complete study of the problem.

Voronskii, A. "I. Babel'." In *Literaturno-kriticheskie stat'i* (Critical articles). Moscow: Sovetskii pisatel', 1963, 274–99. An intelligent if somewhat discursive essay. Voronskii, a Marxist-humanist and editor of the outstanding journal *Krasnaia nov'* (Red virgin soil), where much of Babel's work was published, is defending him against politically motivated attacks. The reader may gain insight into the polemics of the twenties.

Index

DATE DUE

GAYLORD			PRINTED IN U.S.A.